ADVANCE PRAISE FOR

SKIPPING CHURCH

by SUZANNE KELSEY

In *Skipping Church*, Suzanne Kelsey eloquently and honestly describes the challenges of being a minister's spouse and the struggles and rewards of her own search for truth. Her exploration of the complex terrain of a long and loving marriage provides a model for anyone who loves someone with different life goals. Even more, her keen insights, willingness to ask hard questions, and openness to the mysteries and wonders of the world show us that spirituality can be found in many forms.

—LORI ERICKSON, author of *The Soul of the Family Tree: Ancestors, Stories, and the Spirits We Inherit*; *Near the Exit: Travels with the Not-so-Grim Reaper*; and *Holy Rover: Journeys in Search of Mystery, Miracles, and God*

Suzanne Kelsey is a wise guide for those of us who have spiritual stirrings but feel unsure about organized religion. This is her account of arriving at a hard-earned inner harmony. Determined to not fake it as a minister's wife yet to be faithful to her loving husband, she becomes a true soulmate for him and, thankfully, for us too.

—TIM BASCOM, author of *Chameleon Days*; *Running to the Fire*; and *Climbing Lessons: Stories of Fathers, Sons, and the Bond Between*

I can only admire the work of a small-town Iowa woman who embarks on such a profound lifelong spiritual quest and finds its greatest fulfillment in her natural surroundings, wherever they be. Her sharp prose keyed me in to the world of her husband's itinerant ministerial career, something that I at first thought would interest me little. However, her search and how it figured as key to her growing family's dynamic carried me along willingly from town to town to learn what her adventure would unearth. We can all take clues and inspiration from Suzanne Kelsey's story.

—TIM FAY, editor of the *Wapsipinicon Almanac*

With deep honesty, vulnerability, a mystic's sensibility and a keen writer's eye, Sue Kelsey depicts her struggle to create a thoughtful and fiercely independent approach to spiritual life, and find her place in the world, a place of both love and resistance. I come from a family of Midwestern Protestant ministers, and the tension between the roles we are called to play and the authentic self we long to express rings so true here to me. A beautiful book.

—ANDY DOUGLAS, author of *The Curve of the World: Into the Spiritual Heart of Yoga* and *Redemption Songs: A Year in the Life of a Community Prison Choir*

Suzanne Kelsey's engaging memoir brings us on a journey far beyond managing a surprising and sometimes difficult spousal career choice. In seeking her own identity and spirituality separate from her husband's Christian ministry, Kelsey inspires us to understand how art, music, writing, and nature open us to the world's beauty and meaning. The prairies and woodlands of her native Midwest, then new explorations in California landscapes, provide Kelsey and her readers with deep insight into the power of nature to make us who we are in our home landscapes as well as the greater universe—and how they can bring family members together in a loving common life.

—THOMAS DEAN, author of *Under a Midland Sky*, co-author of *Tallgrass Conversations: In Search of the Prairie Spirit*

How do you respect the spiritual calling of a loved one, while listening to your own? This is the question that drives Suzanne Kelsey's remarkable memoir, an unexpected journey of faith that leads her to discover "startling revelations of beauty" beyond the walls of a church. Whether during walks in nature, learning to tango, protesting a polluting factory, or confronting the complexities of marriage and parenting, Kelsey's honesty and warmth are always present. As well as her exceptional gifts as a storyteller, as she uncovers sacred connections "to the wild, to history, to beauty, to creativity, and community." An inspiring, essential read in these challenging times.

—JOHN T. PRICE, author of *Daddy Long Legs: The Natural Education of a Father* and *Man Killed by Pheasant and Other Kinships*

SKIPPING CHURCH

SKIPPING CHURCH
notes from an accidental minister's wife

SUZANNE KELSEY

SHANTI ARTS PUBLISHING
BRUNSWICK, MAINE

Skipping Church
Notes from an Accidental Minister's Wife

Published by Shanti Arts Publishing

Cover and interior design by Shanti Arts Designs

Cover artwork by Suzanne Kelsey;
used with her permission

Shanti Arts LLC
Brunswick, Maine
www.shantiarts.com

Printed in the United States of America

ISBN: 978-1-956056-07-5 (softcover)
ISBN: 978-1-956056-08-2 (digital)

Library of Congress Control Number: 2021946452

To Chuck
my VIP dance partner
my best friend
my love

Contents

Acknowledgements

THANK YOU TO THE MANY PEOPLE WHO HAVE GIVEN FEEDBACK
to parts of this manuscript over the years, beginning with the
dozens of my students at Kirkwood Community College who
patiently workshopped a couple early chapters just as seriously as
they did their peers' writing. Other people who responded to early
work include Hope Burwell, Sue Futrell, Kate Gleason, Jennifer
New, Marjorie Carlson Davis, Allison York, Robert Dana, and
Peg Dana.

Without the generosity of Joan Drury, co-creator of
Norcroft, a women's writing retreat near Lutsen, Minnesota, I
might never have had the courage to call myself a Writer with
a capital W. Joan is recently departed, but her spirit surely
lives on in the hundreds of women who were lucky enough to
call Norcroft home for a few weeks. I am also grateful to the
Norcroft writers who listened to me read some of my material
and offered encouragement. Special thanks to Betsey Norland
and Kara Lee Corthron, who, post-Norcroft, graciously offered
feedback on an early draft of the book.

Marjorie Carlson Davis, Claudia Bischoff, and Joyce
Daniels deserve credit for the heavy-lifting literary help as
they urged me to further dig in, develop, shape, and polish the
material. Thank you from the bottom of my heart to these dear
friends and writing colleagues with whom I am forever bonded.
I treasure the hours we've spent together over the years, talking
and writing and laughing and critiquing together at George's
and Formosa and our homes in Iowa City, Sanibel, and Mason
City. Our dear Joyce is no longer with us, but I can hear her
indomitable spirit encouraging the rest of us forward and
reminding us to celebrate every single day.

My thank-yous also go to Barbara O'Rourke, Randy Poole,
Linda Rice, Diane and Steve Clark, Michele Welter, Barb
Waite, Andy Douglas, Laurie and Dave Waite, Pat Lehnherr,
Kelly Poole, Madeline Shelby, and Emily Weil for their support

and encouragement of this project. I also leaned on Thomas Dean's excellent editing skills for the chapters "Leaving Home" and "River City Wild."

In the end, editor Dan Weeks helped me pull it all together. Dan, I can't thank you enough. You are the best editor ever, and you came into my writing life at just the right time.

As did Christine Brooks Cote and Shanti Arts Publishing. When I read that Shanti Arts is "driven by a passion for nature, for art, for beauty, for significance," I hoped I'd found a home for my manuscript. I'm so glad they took me in. Thank you, Christine. Thanks also goes to Gretchen Kauffman for her fine copyediting skills.

I owe my heartfelt thanks to my mother, Evelyn Pierce, who has always encouraged my self-expression, whether it be through playing the clarinet, making art, or writing. Mom, you knew me well before I did. I love you dearly. My dad, John Pierce, also supported me in his quiet way. Thank you, Dad. I miss you.

Other VIP friends and family members have also offered so much loving support over the years as I have wrestled with the mantle of "minister's wife" and with the moves required by Chuck's work. I especially thank my siblings, Fran Pierce Oppold and Joe Pierce, and their mates, Frank Oppold and Marty Pierce. I also thank in-laws Marji and Paul Zani and Mary and Jim Martz.

There are so many other friends who have encouraged me as I've made my awkward and slow transitions from place to place. I see it all much more clearly now—the relay teams of support as people from the old places checked in with us as we moved to the new places—even as angels from the new places, in the form of parishioners and other townspeople, welcomed us in. I'll leave too many out if I try to name names. I hope you know who you are. I love and appreciate you all.

Jesse, Keegan, Melanie, Natasha, Finn, Liam, and Ashoka, what can I say? I love you all so much. Thank you for your undying support and your many expressions of love. Keep being exactly who you are. Everyone should be so lucky to have such an amazing family.

To Charles—my muse, my #1 fan, my favorite companion, my love: What a ride it's been.

I hope it continues for a long, long time.

✳

The author also wishes to acknowledge the editors of the following publications in which some chapters of this book were previously published:

CityTalk (Chicago), Chapter 10, "Quiet Desperation" published as "Living a Life of Simplicity," June 8, 2001

Mom Writer's Literary Magazine, Chapter 15, "New Lives," June 2008

Spirituality and Health, Chapter 17, "Exile," published as "Learning to Bloom Where I am Planted," January/February 2017; Chapter 21, "It Takes Two," published as "It Takes Two: Taking Time for Alchemy in a Marriage," November, 2020

Troika Magazine, Chapter 9, "Sax and Sartre," Fall 1998; Chapter 10, "Quiet Desperation" published as "Voluntary Simplicity: An Alternative to Prozac," Fall 2000

Wapsipinicon Almanac, Chapter 13, "The Nature of Disturbance," #14, December 2007; Chapter 19, "River City Wild," #25, December 2018

CHAPTER 1

The Proclamation

1989

"Sit down a minute, will you, Suz?" Chuck gestured at the sofa in the living room.

It was early December 1989. Vegetable soup simmered in the kitchen; our sons, Jesse and Keegan, ten and six, played with LEGOs in their bedroom. I looked at my dark-haired mate, his brown eyes as serious as I'd ever seen in our fourteen years of marriage. He was usually clowning for us, dancing the faux-salsa or pushing his glasses down his nose, like Jerry Lewis in *The Nutty Professor.*

He sat next to me, his thigh touching mine.

Was he sick?

"I can't keep avoiding it. That old tug to be a minister. I've tried not to pay attention, but it keeps coming back. I feel I am called to work in the Methodist Church."

The smell of the soup suddenly nauseated me. I moved a few inches away. I thought we'd settled this well before we married. Was he breaking the deal?

"But what about the counseling degree?" I asked. Chuck was two weeks from finishing a bachelor's in psychology at the University of Iowa and had been accepted into a master's program in counseling.

He took my hands; his were clammy. "Counseling and ministry are different. I want to be a minister."

We were thirty-three. The year before, we'd moved to the Iowa City/Coralville area from Iowa Falls, our rural hometown in north central Iowa, so Chuck could finish college and I could find a decent-paying job with my new master's degree in English.

I finally felt like a grown-up with my first professional job as an editor at ACT, the testing company. Our two-bedroom apartment felt luxurious after ten years of living in a tiny house in the country. On days off we listened to jazz and blues at the downtown pedestrian mall while our boys played hide-and-seek on a wooden playground. We packed family picnics, biked all over the city, swam at the apartment pool, made new friends. After dark, I ran and danced around the neighborhood with my Walkman, listening to Gloria Estefan and the Miami Sound Machine.

Life was so good.

"But I don't like church," I wailed. Since moving to Coralville, we'd sporadically attended a Methodist church at Chuck's request. "I don't want to be trapped in a dark sanctuary on Sunday mornings. And I don't want to live my life in a fishbowl."

"You don't have to," Chuck said. "Churches are changing what they expect from ministers' wives, or at least they should. I'm called to do this. I know it's not your calling."

"But the Methodists move their ministers around. We'll have to leave Iowa City."

"Not as often as they used to. Anyway, it'll take me several years to finish seminary. I'll go summers to Garrett Seminary, near Chicago. They have a program for midlife career changers, so we'll be able to stay here while I'm in school. And I've talked to the pastor at Coralville Methodist. He says I can work there part-time."

"I guess you have it all figured out," I sputtered.

The tension in our voices drew the boys to the living room. Jess asked softly, "Can we play Monopoly?" Silently, Chuck and I set up the board, our sons watching our faces. Keegan's blue eyes were wide; Jesse's brown eyes darted from us to the board as he put the yellow Chance cards in place. Chuck and I played the game mechanically.

For weeks after our talk, I protested whenever the boys weren't underfoot. But he had clearly thought through the decision and was now gently but stubbornly braced for backlash. And underneath my pleading arguments, I knew I could not be the reason Chuck wasn't answering his calling.

I just wasn't sure our marriage would survive.

I'm an independent, freethinking introvert. I sense a divine something-or-other in Midwest prairies and woods, but I do not subscribe to organized religion. I value my privacy, but the ministers' wives I'd observed in my youth in Iowa Falls seemed like silent, smiling appendages to their husbands. Some years later I learned that one reportedly told friends, in so many words, that preachers' wives could eat but not defecate and they could have babies but not fornicate.

I wanted to put roots down in Iowa City, but Chuck's decision would mean moving away. It felt like Chuck was choosing an itinerant, public life of commitment to doctrine for both of us—a life in which some parishioners would expect me to be his partner in ministry. I wanted no part of that strange world.

I felt sad, angry, and abandoned as he became licensed to preach, served as a part-time associate pastor at the Coralville church, and began summer classes at Garrett–Evangelical Theological Seminary, four hours away on the campus of Northwestern University in Evanston. But Chuck was determined, and because I loved him, I could not stand in the way.

Our reality soon included phone calls from parishioners in the middle of the night. Chuck's evening and weekend church meetings left me to single parent much of the time as our family's needs took second place over the busy church schedule. No more dancing in the dark around the neighborhood—the boys were too young to be left alone at home.

Sure enough, Chuck's supervising minister told him I would ruin his career if I didn't participate. Even though long walks in the woods around the Coralville Reservoir filled my soul much more on Sunday mornings than sitting in a pew, with a sinking heart I did my best to be a visible clergy spouse. I taught Sunday school classes and coaxed the boys to attend church with me at least twice a month.

I felt sidelined, invisible, derailed. I felt guilty when I skipped church, resentful when I went.

Relatives and friends from our hometown enthusiastically supported Chuck, peppering him with questions about his work when they visited. Delighted with his new status, his older relatives began addressing letters to us as "The Reverend and Mrs. Charles Kelsey," though he was years away from being fully ordained. I cringed when Chuck's mother gave him a set of handkerchiefs for Christmas "to offer to the ladies when they cry." Was he going to be a surrogate husband for any women in need just because he had morphed like a superhero into a minister?

Even my piano teacher saw me as Pastor Chuck's sidekick. The boys and I were all under her instruction. She was a small, frail woman in her late sixties. Due to childhood polio, she walked with a cane. She had white hair in a bun enclosed by a white net, but her face was virtually unlined. Mrs. Shepardson was a good teacher with a traditional approach: scales, finger exercises, and classical arrangements appropriate to our skills. The boys made decent progress with beginners' books; I began to master pieces like "Minute Waltz."

Janet Oakes Christian novels were stacked on our piano teacher's coffee table; wall plaques advertised Bible verses. She made laminated placemats from green- and white-striped computer paper on which she pasted scenic pictures from old calendars and calligraphed verses from Psalms. She flipped past certain pages in the boys' beginners' books. "I don't think this song is pleasing to the Lord," she said about "The Spider Dance," "Elfin Night," and "Goblin Rag." At home, I encouraged them to play the forbidden songs with the snappier beats.

She introduced me to other students' parents with "This is Mrs. Kelsey, the wife of the Methodist minister Chuck Kelsey."

Mrs. Shepardson told me that the Lord was leading her to teach me how to play chords on the organ. "My minister's wife is so good at picking up any old hymn, and I know you could do that too," she said. I told her I didn't like the sound of organs, but it didn't matter; every week she said, "I'm praying for you, Mrs. Kelsey. I think I'm supposed to teach you those chords. Why don't you give the organ a try?"

Expectations and misperceptions continued to pop up everywhere like spring mushrooms. Strangers stiffened and altered their language when they learned Chuck was a minister. With the invisible but ever-present "Ask me what I do" bumper sticker on his forehead in those days, it usually didn't take long for them to find out.

In church, it felt unnatural to listen to the head pastor or Chuck tell me how to think. I made myself attend adult study groups, appreciating the liberal thinkers but mystified by the literalists and those few who talked about Jesus like he was a romantic partner. Kathleen Norris wrote in *Dakota: A Spiritual Geography* that when she returned to the church after years of absence, she often sped home afterward to lie down for several hours because of the jarring Christian rhetoric. I, too, needed only to hear someone say, "Jesus is my beloved," to feel like assuming a fetal position.

I contemplated quitting piano lessons. It was one thing I could quit during that time of turmoil. The boys were restless too. I felt Mrs. Shepardson corrected them too often when they played. When they started chanting, "It's-not-pleasing-to-the-Lord," on the way home from lessons, I decided it was time to bail. I told Mrs. Shepardson we needed a break. She said she'd pray for all of us.

In those early years of Chuck's ministry, I often thought about a novel by Willa Cather that I'd read in a college literature class: *My Antonia*, set in Nebraska in the early 1900s. Narrator Jim Burden visits his childhood friend, Antonia, who lives in the country with her family. Burden sees that Antonia's husband would rather live in the city as a musician and farms only because it is Antonia's dream. Burden muses, "I wondered whether the life that was right for one was ever right for two."

I often wondered the same thing, having accidentally become married to a minister. Was the life right for one ever right for two?

Was I always going to have to lip sync my way through the Lord's Prayer?

Must I live in Chuck's shadow or could I follow my calling too? And if I could, what was it? Surely not editing test items.

Where would "home" be as we moved at the Iowa Methodist bishop's whim from city to city, congregation to congregation, parsonage to parsonage?

Was the life right for one ever right for two?

I was not at all sure.

CHAPTER 2

Insignificant as Algebra

1967–74

FALL 1967   A HUNDRED FIFTH GRADERS FROM ACROSS the town of Iowa Falls gathered once a week to play simple march and classical tunes in a room that doubled as a cafeteria and smelled of goulash and pre-adolescent sweat. I was all business in the clarinet section. Back in percussion, a somber girl named Stephanie, future high school friend, hit the bass drum in perfect time. But the rest of the percussion players were goof-offs. The snare drummers, led by a boy named Chuck, took over the tempo—deliberately, it seemed—drumming their off-beats too soon after Stephanie's downbeats. We stopped and started our way through the pieces, the director constantly rapping his pointed baton on the metal stand.

The jerky pace frustrated me, but when Chuck's disruptions caused the horns to fizzle, all I could do was turn around and giggle, like the other girls.

He was cute.

Large dimples formed when he smiled, and thick brown hair fell into his eyes, early-Beatles style. Twice-daily workouts milking cows made him as solid and muscular as a twelve-year-old boy could be.

In ninth grade, hoping to keep my lead in the clarinet section the next year in high school, I faithfully practiced scales and band music, placing my fingers just right to keep the notes pure and true. I studied my lines for the school play and wrote notebooks full of prefeminist poetry, often centered on Chuck, my secret crush:

My king
Doesn't know
That he rules over me.
He walks by,
unknowing, unfeeling.
Someday
I will be
his queen.

Tenth grade, our first class together. Retaining little about photosynthesis and DNA, I could only concentrate on the tingling sensation in the back of my neck as Chuck Kelsey, who sat behind me, aimed wisecracks my way. "Hey, Pierce, would you stand up? Oh, you are standing. How tall are you anyway?"

"Tall enough to tell you to mind your own business. Four feet, eleven and a quarter." I grinned at Deb, my friend and lab partner. She and I wore low-waisted hip-hugger jeans with the wide bottoms. Elephant pants, we called them.

Finally, what I'd been waiting for: Chuck's phone call. "Will you go to the Christmas dance with me tomorrow night?"

"Yes, I'd like that," I whispered into the phone, my parents looking on, their eyebrows raised.

After all the flirting in biology class, Chuck and I were tongue-tied in the old high school gym decorated with Christmas trees and lights. To cover our awkward silence, we danced all evening, "Hey Jude" giving us an excuse to touch each other, our bodies fitting together nicely despite a ten-inch difference in height. I lay my head against his broad shoulder. His English Leather mingled with my Wind Song. Friends twirled by, winking and nodding.

Chuck gave me a black-and-white wrestling photograph, which I pinned to my bulletin board at home, glancing often at the muscular curve of his biceps. I went weak when I saw him in the halls.

He wrote me love poems and said hello to everyone,

regardless of their size, shape, or popularity. When a classmate became pregnant our junior year and most of us didn't know what to say, Chuck congratulated her, showing the rest of us by example how to be supportive.

The poems, the flowers—the spring after that Christmas dance, he gave them to me freely and often. "Mrs. G. won't miss these from her garden," he'd say, pulling two daffodils from behind his back. It threw me a little, the sensitivity. Later it would become one of the qualities I loved most about him, but to my adolescent brain, he just seemed a little strange. Weren't boys supposed to be strong and macho? He was strong from all those years of farm work, but macho?

Stranger still, he was active in his Methodist church youth group, even attending statewide meetings and helping run summer church camps. He and his family lived in the country next door to his grandparents, who took Chuck and his sisters to church. They'd all drawn strength there after Chuck's oldest sister died of cancer when he was six. Even after his grandparents died, Chuck continued to attend the church his ancestors had helped establish decades earlier.

My family attended a Congregational church on the mornings my mother could cajole my father, brother, sister, and me to dress up and pile in the old Rambler, its rusty floorboards punctured here and there by Mom's high heels. If the minister gave sermons about grace and love, I don't remember them; I only registered fire and brimstone. By fourth grade, I doubted I could believe in a squinty-eyed God who watched my every move.

One Sunday after Reverend H. preached about accountability, I asked my mother, "When will God start deciding I'm accountable for the things I do?"

"Oh, by age twelve or so," Mom said casually.

I had a couple of years. I sighed with relief.

In ninth grade, I attended confirmation classes to please my parents. Wearing the requisite white robe and white pumps, I mumbled my vows, but I wasn't any closer to believing in God.

I didn't like church. Why sit in a dark sanctuary on a beautiful Sunday morning when you could be outdoors? Who gave the preacher the right to be an authority on God and tell the rest of us how to think? Church—who needed it?

In tenth grade, after learning about the word "atheist," I decided the category fit me. Chuck and I had friendly disagreements over our beliefs, and though I didn't understand his enthusiasm for the church, we tolerated each other's perspectives.

We were young and in love. Our theological differences were as insignificant as algebra.

In high school I checked groceries at the SuperValu wearing high wedge sandals and a royal blue minidress uniform. Pre-barcode days, I punched the prices on a cash register. My parents worked hard, Mom as a bookkeeper at a local bank and Dad in the order department of Ralston Purina, a feed mill. But with college costs ahead, I worked as many hours as I could—Monday evenings, Saturdays, and every other Sunday from 8 a.m. to 11 p.m. I dreaded those long Sundays, but I liked the satisfying click of the keys and prided myself on the same accuracy and agility I had with the clarinet. Sometimes after watching my hands fly, elderly customers would eagle-eye the receipt, then smile and nod and gather the packages.

When I heard the rumble of a motorcycle, I knew Chuck might soon be leaning on my counter in his black leather jacket, hair tickling his shoulders, his purchase always the same: a Three Musketeers bar with a quarter on top, his finger gripping the money so I had to pry it away.

Chuck's father ran a Harley-Davidson dealership on the family farm in the days before Harley big-box stores. Chuck rode a 350 Sprint, a new model Harley billed as the "Great American Machine," he proudly told me. He'd earned the bike in exchange for labor at the shop. We rode around the county, our bodies nestled close, my arms around his waist. Sometimes we wore helmets, but mostly we let the wind comb our hair. Whenever he roared into our driveway, my parents' jaws went tight with worry. While Chuck had grown up playing cowboys and Indians with his sisters on ponies and motorcycles, my upbringing was tuned more to avoiding dangers than seeking thrills. But my parents never complained about Chuck. They liked him.

One May evening at dusk near the end of our senior year, we motorcycled around town, Chuck leaning hard into the curves, me sitting upright, afraid of tipping. "Lean with me!" he yelled.

"You're going too fast!"

"Just hang on. It's okay!"

We rode to the corner of the downtown park. I climbed off the bike and bought a five-cent bag of popcorn. The owner of the little stand smiled and handed me the brown bag. I ambled toward a picnic table. The bike started up again; I turned and saw Chuck easing out of the angled parking. "Watch this!" He accelerated for a block, then stood on the seat while the bike zipped forward. His arms in a T for balance, he yelled, "Woohooh!" I glanced warily at the police station across the street, but no cops came running. Chuck returned, grinning, his hair blown into cowlicks.

"Wanna try it?" he yelled.

I shook my head.

He dismounted and took some popcorn, shaking it in one hand as if he were mining for gold, then throwing it in his mouth. He wiped his hand on his jeans. "Come on, let's go."

I hesitated, then climbed on the noisy bike. As Chuck accelerated, I clutched his jacket, yelling, "Slow down!"

"Trust me, baby!" He wiggled his back against me for reassurance.

We rode a half mile to the junior high that overlooked the Iowa River. Chuck waved at a few high school boys. "Hang on!" he said, and then he was zooming up the steep, grassy hill behind the school. At the top, the bike flew several feet into the air and landed, hard, our bodies thumping on the narrow seat a couple seconds later. The boys waved and whooped. "Way to go, Kelsey!"

"Let me off!" I yelled

He stopped the bike, chuckling. "It's okay."

"No, it's not." I jumped off.

"Okay, okay," he said. "No more tricks. I promise. Climb on." His brown eyes were soft.

I nodded. "Okay, but remember, you promised."

He slowly drove to my house in the cool spring air. My parents offered him a lemonade.

1973   We became engaged at eighteen, the summer before college. None of our parents objected. Mine were pleased we were going to college; Chuck's assumed he'd take a year or two of school and then return to work for his dad at the Harley shop. I wanted to head on down to the University of Iowa to become one of the Vietnam War-protesting, flower-powering hippies I'd seen on television. But it made more practical sense to save money by living at home and attending the local junior college on scholarships. In August Chuck left for Morningside, a Methodist college three hours away in Sioux City, selling his Sprint to help pay tuition. The engagement was our effort to make things stay the same, even as we went separate ways.

Barely a month into the semester, Chuck phoned. "I think I want to be a minister, Suz. Last summer I really felt the presence of God."

I held my breath as I sat at the kitchen table. He'd spent the summer in Tennessee as a volunteer for the Methodist-sponsored Appalachia Service Project, a home-repair service. But career ministry had never occurred to me.

How people decided to be ministers had never crossed my mind.

"One night I was sitting by a candle, and I asked God for a sign if I should be a minister. The light flared up right then—a huge burst—but I didn't trust it. And I knew you wouldn't like it, so I didn't say anything. But now with this religion class I'm taking, I'm excited. I'm pretty sure I want to do it."

My throat tightened. I gripped the phone with one hand and scratched our miniature schnauzer's silky ears with the other. She tilted her salt-and-pepper head. How could I be supportive to Chuck when I didn't even like church?

I couldn't.

"You should do this if you need to," I responded. "But I can't marry a minister. It's not the life for me. I'll give you back the ring." I held my breath, hoping he'd say, "Okay, I'll forget it." But he didn't.

In several weeks, the Iowa Falls Methodist Church held a service of recognition after Chuck publicly declared his intent to become a minister. I attended, the ex-girlfriend. His parents hadn't initially been enthused about their son going to college, but now they and other extended family members rallied behind him.

Chuck and I spent the rest of the year apart, Carole King's "It's Too Late" and Todd Rundgren's "Hello, It's Me" singing my misery. That fall I found a wooded area on the outskirts of town—a sanctuary just beyond the cemetery, not far from the Iowa River. In a quiet hilltop clearing, I sat on a picnic table ringed by trees, absorbing birdcalls and the smell of dry leaves. Until it was too cold that season I returned to read, do homework, write poems, and watch the oaks and ashes go bronze and gold. I sat in the womb of this quiet space, unselfconscious and content in these woods, however much in turmoil otherwise.

Nature connected me to something centering in a way church didn't. I could take off the masks of politeness I wore for school or work. I could just be.

And think. About my three-year relationship with Chuck but about other things too. My junior college teachers were introducing me to the life of the mind. When they mentioned writers in class, I checked out their books from the college library. Reading *Lysistrata*, I discovered people had been cynical about wars centuries before Vietnam, unlike Joe, my patriotic, World War II-veteran boss at the jewelry store. I acted in *The Night Thoreau Spent in Jail*, read *Walden*, resonating with Thoreau's close ties to nature. Inspired by my English teacher, I checked out a book of criticism about William Carlos Williams; I, too, came to believe that "so much depends upon a red wheelbarrow"—that aesthetics can be as transcending to us as religion. My art teacher taught me to paint feeling instead of reality. When my English professor teased me about wanting to keep one of my fuchsia and yellow paintings of abstract people dancing, I flushed with pride.

At Ellsworth Junior College I explored the new world of ideas and books, took classes, worked at the jewelry store, dated a few boys who just made me miss Chuck more, and partied on the weekends with my best friends, Deb and Stephanie. The drinking age was eighteen in respect for Vietnam soldiers who could die for their country and should therefore be able to drink. We spent Friday nights drinking Tom Collins cocktails at the Crazy Eight. One night a naked streaker with a gorilla mask entered the front door on a motorcycle and raced out the back.

When I wasn't partying or studying or working, I incubated in the Ira Nichols Bird Refuge, the slice of nature on the edge of town.

SPRING 1974 It was the end of our freshman year of college. Chuck appeared at my house on a Saturday evening. He wore a flannel shirt and jeans and with his hair in a ponytail, he was more handsome than ever. He reached for a hug, but I stepped back. I would not be seduced. I would not be a minister's wife.

We walked upstairs to the living room and sat on opposite ends of the sofa.

"Suz, I just want you to know something."

I waited, glancing downstairs to see if my parents or brother had come up from the family room to eavesdrop from the foyer. No one was there.

"I've decided not to be a minister." Chuck watched my face.

I looked out the living room window at the new leaves on the locust tree. "Why?"

"It's just not right for me after all. I'm changing my major to psychology. I like my psych class now. It's a better fit."

With my finger I traced an image on the cover of my mother's *Better Homes & Gardens* on the maple coffee table. "Does this decision have something to do with me? Because if it does . . ."

"No. Really. It's not about you. I liked the idea, but then it felt like everybody except you was suddenly too excited. I started to feel pushed, especially by Mom, and then I didn't want to do it anymore." I thought about the party at the church the previous fall.

The few boys I dated that year had not matched Chuck's sensitivity, his casual, accepting manner. In contrast to my quick temper, I'd rarely seen him angry in the three years we'd dated. I couldn't imagine being as deeply connected to someone as I was to Chuck. I touched his flannel shirt. His sleeves were rolled up, revealing those strong forearms. I inhaled his English Leather and whispered, "Want to go for pizza?"

The bad dream was suddenly over. He'd gotten the idea out of his system, and I had nothing to do with it. That's what he said.

CHAPTER 3

Cognitive Dissonance

1974-88

FALL 1974 I TURNED THE DEFINITION OF "COGNITIVE dissonance" over in my mind while walking from the stately Pentacrest at the University of Iowa to the modern English-Philosophy Building down the hill, near the Iowa River—the same river that runs through Iowa Falls, three hours north and west.

"Cognitive dissonance: discomfort or ambivalence experienced by someone who holds two or more contradictory beliefs or ideas or is confronted with new information that conflicts with existing beliefs or ideas."

Just a few weeks into classes my sophomore year, my first year at the U of I, I was already in love with the learning, the campus, Iowa City. All of it.

This was the place for me.

We'd just learned about cognitive dissonance in a social psychology class. As I headed to my women's lit class, I was already applying the concept to a character in a Marge Piercy novel we were reading. Wasn't the cognitive dissonance experienced by the two main characters the subject of the novel, its reason for being?

I was making these interdisciplinary connections almost every day. It was exhilarating.

And I was free. Free of small-town scrutiny. I could be anyone I wanted, given the constraints of taking a full course load and working my way through college.

I was meeting interesting people through my work, first as

an engraver at a jewelry store and then a waitress at Howard Johnson's on the east edge of town. One night I waited on the entire Boston Philharmonic Orchestra after its evening gig at Hancher Auditorium. I became friends with a woman named Sally, in her sixties, who came to the restaurant frequently and told me enthusiastically about pursuing her MFA program in art at the university.

Maybe I wasn't as carefree as most of my sorority sisters whose college expenses were paid by their parents. They played bridge and flag football, watched M*A*S*H reruns, and wore their Kappa t-shirts while drinking at the Airliner. Still, I enjoyed my quiet study periods and late-night discussions with roommates.

Chuck joined me in Iowa City that January. The next January, the middle of our junior year and at the age of twenty, defying the negative statistics for high school sweethearts, we got married. By then we were both working full-time to pay for college and expenses; it made economic sense to pool our resources. After all, two could live more cheaply than one. That's what everyone said.

Yes, we would miss living with our friends. And yes, he was religious and I wasn't.

Cognitive dissonance—there was plenty of it.

I ignored it.

Friends and family members filled the Methodist church in Iowa Falls on our wedding night—the coldest one that January. Then we headed back to school in Iowa City. Chuck worked as a mechanic for the city and I as a ward clerk at the University of Iowa Hospitals. I proceeded to finish my bachelor's degree in general studies, with an emphasis in women's studies, literature, and social psychology. I especially liked essay-writing classes. Essays were a way to play with ideas and make sense of things—of life. It was exciting to share my writing with a dozen classmates and an encouraging professor, and my work at the hospital gave me plenty to write about.

A year and a half after our wedding, I had my degree but no clue what to do next. I only knew I loved ideas and literature and writing. Chuck had fizzled out on his degree, no longer sure about a psychology major, and dropped out. But he knew exactly what he wanted.

"I want to go back to Iowa Falls and work with Dad. I know

he doesn't have the Harley shop anymore since he refused to move it to town, but I think I could help him develop the auto salvage into a really good business."

My heart sank at the thought of returning to Iowa Falls. It was 1978. We were twenty-three.

"Steel prices are good, so we can make good money on scrapping." Chuck's brown eyes were intense. "We can live in the little house down the road from Mom and Dad."

"So close to your parents?" I pictured the house on a hill that overlooked a soybean field and, beyond, the Iowa River valley. It was a scenic spot, but I couldn't imagine living a quarter mile from my in-laws, even as easy-going as they were.

And I didn't want to leave Iowa City, my place of books and ideas and creativity.

Yet it was true: I had no vision for a career beyond the rote work I was doing as a ward clerk.

Chuck, at least, had a vision.

Me? I was just full of cognitive dissonance.

Before the move, I wrote up a contract for Chuck to sign: We would save two hundred dollars each month for future getaway plans. I secretly didn't intend to stay in Iowa Falls very long, a year at most. The contract stipulated that he would not get involved in the church—wouldn't teach Sunday school, lead the youth group, or any other such volunteering. He hadn't brought up being a minister since our freshman year, but I certainly didn't want to revisit that conversation. He smiled, hugged me for reassurance, and signed. "I'll be too tied up with the business to get involved anyway," he said. I packed my diploma, worried I would find it useless, especially in rural Iowa. We moved our belongings in a van and a faded blue Chevy Impala.

In Iowa Falls, within six months Chuck began teaching Sunday School. I struggled to find work but eventually began working part-time as a newspaper typesetter, then became pregnant. After a few years, the farm crisis and low metal prices caused Chuck's income to drop by three-quarters. For extra cash, he became a part-time youth director at the Iowa Falls Methodist Church.

We saved no money.

We stayed ten years.

There were bright spots during our ten years in Iowa Falls. The lush view of the Iowa River valley from our tiny two-bedroom house on a hill. Motherhood and its daily miracles, like our boys' first giggles—Jess lying on the bed in his fuzzy yellow sleeper, laughter tinkling while Chuck gently tickled him; Keegan, wild-haired, belly laughing, and kicking his legs inside his forest green velour robe.

There was also my gradual shift to at least entertaining the idea of a loving God. I remembered William James's point in his essay "The Will to Believe" that there's no proof that "dupery though hope is so much worse than dupery through fear," and that "religion is a live hypothesis which may be true." It was hardly an unqualified endorsement of faith, but it made sense that choosing to believe might offer more gain than loss. I began to pray and listen for an inner, divine voice while walking in the pasture or woods by myself.

As I watched our sons grow, and as the Iowa River valley seasons turned from white to celery, then gold and bronze, my awe at the divine artist's creative power grew ever stronger, even if I still felt constrained inside a church when Chuck talked me into going.

More challenging for me were the vocational dead ends. Iowa Falls was a man's town. It was mostly men who ran the businesses and the Chamber of Commerce. They were the doctors, dentists, lawyers, and surgeons. Decisions were made by men over drinks at the Elks. Women worked as teachers, nurses, clerks, or secretaries. My lot was telephone sales at a veterinary supply company, where I developed a reputation as a mouthy little feminist.

In the early 1980s, Hayden Fry, football coach of the University of Iowa, was trying to cultivate sympathy for the busy life of Division I athletes. He said that when he was a young athlete, he could count on a coed—"some little dumpling"—to do his laundry. News of university feminists dressing him down made its way across the state. That year at the Christmas party, my grinning boss presented me with a t-shirt on behalf of his cronies that said, "One of Hayden's Little Dumplings."

I made a funny comeback and played the good sport. I never wore the shirt.

One day on the steps of the post office, I ran into the wife of a community college English professor I'd had twelve years earlier.

"What are you doing these days?" she asked.

"Selling pig medicine," I said, rolling my eyes.

"Sue, you were one of Dan's favorite students. Think about commuting to Iowa State for a master's in English. You could be a teaching assistant while you get your degree. They'd pay you a stipend plus your tuition—probably close to what you're paid now. It would only be two years, and then you could teach at a community college. They're all over the state."

It was the lifeline I needed. I applied to Iowa State and began the hour commute three days a week, teaching first-year composition while taking coursework. I felt energized, immersed in rhetorical theory and pedagogical strategies for teaching college writing. After I graduated, ACT in Iowa City offered me the editorial position. It wasn't teaching, but it was a professional job with good pay and benefits. I thought life had given us—given me—a second chance.

Life was so good.

Until that proclamation.

CHAPTER 4

The Bitch

1990

THE CALL TO WORSHIP BEGAN AS SOON AS WE SAT DOWN AT the restaurant.

"Very nice service, Chuck," Jack offered. A farmer, his cheeks were ruddy and his forehead baby-bottom white from years of wearing a seed-corn cap in the sun.

"Yes, Chuck," chimed Elise. "Beautiful. How many were there today?"

"About a hundred."

Elise raised feathered eyebrows in approval. "That's great for a new congregation. You've only been going a few months. You're so new to the ministry!"

My relatives, distant cousins of my parents, had traveled from Iowa Falls to attend Chuck's Sunday service. The Iowa Methodist Conference had tapped him even before finishing seminary to start a new church in Iowa City. The congregation rented space from a Korean Methodist church, a steeple-topped ranch-style building. Chuck's parishioners met early, then ambled out, greeting Korean university students and faculty who carried spring rolls and jars of kimchi for lunch after their service.

Older colleagues warned Chuck he'd been chosen because he was cheap labor—indeed, my salary was doing the heavy lifting—and expendable. New churches rarely survived, they said, and he would be blamed for any failure. But Chuck was unflappable and pleased to be selected. And now relatives and friends were visiting us in twos and threes from Iowa Falls and other places to see the church for themselves and offer Chuck their support.

And adulation.

At the restaurant, Jess and Keegan blew the papers off their straws and drew cartoons on placemats. The inquiry continued. "How many members in the church?" "Does it have a women's group?" "What do you do about Sunday school?" "How many other Methodist Churches are there in the city?"

Chuck's brown eyes glowed as he answered this familiar litany of questions. Half-listening, I focused on a light bulb in the distance, staring until it turned into three bulbs, then four, then five. At moments like this I found life as a minister's wife easier lived slightly out of focus.

"Do you ever wear a robe?" Elise asked, her fork poised above her salad.

"Sometimes," Chuck answered. "Mostly at weddings or funerals."

I spoke before I could censor myself. "I can't stand the robe, so I'm glad he doesn't wear it much."

Jess and Keegan looked up. Jack and Elise turned to me with half-smiles. "What?" Elise said.

"His white robe makes him look like a monk." They waited.

"Monks are celibate," I reminded them. Their faces were blank. "And his black robe makes him look officious and self-important. It's like he's wearing costumes for a play."

"Suzie!" Elise reprimanded, like an overbearing parent. "What are you going to do? The congregation will expect Charlie to wear a robe!"

And they're the priority now, aren't they? I thought.

Jack shifted back to Chuck. Jesse and Keegan resumed drawing.

"How long do you think they'll keep you at this church?"

"Quite a few years, I hope," said Chuck.

Another sensitive subject. I stared at the light bulb again, pondering what "quite a few years" might mean. Iowa City had given me my first decent job, our boys an excellent school system, and we finally felt at home. But the bishop could make us move any time.

The conversation with Jack and Elise continued. Finally, Elise turned to me and gushed, "He's always wanted to be a minister. Isn't it nice that he's finally doing it?"

I nodded while the Bitch thought, Yes, isn't it nice.

In those early years of Chuck's ministry, I thought of that part of myself in the third person: the Bitch. Angry and mouthy, she wanted to piss Chuck off, wanted him to suffer because of some decision she would make, derailing his life. She thought about taking up smoking, but she hated the habit. She considered a tattoo, something like "Down with the clergy" or "Pastard Chuck" in Easter-purple letters on her ankle or upper lip. She checked into joining the National Guard; Chuck was a pacifist, so that would get to him. The trouble was, she was a pacifist too. Anyway, they told her she was too old.

She knew these were revenge fantasies, every bit as juvenile as the poems she'd written about unrequited love in junior high. But thirteen-year-old girls are supposed to write juvenile love poems. The problem was, there were no appropriate, legitimate, socially sanctioned ways for the Bitch to express her anger—no traditions, no rituals, no mourning services for new clergy spouses suddenly finding themselves in surreal, Daliesque worlds where people melted prostrate over men in robes. It seemed that everybody—everybody—was rooting for Chuck.

And God was on his side too.

I confessed to a minister's wife in town that I had difficulty listening to Chuck preach. His preacher persona was more theatrical than the private, low-keyed one I loved so much, I said. "He's never that animated at home. And it seems odd to hear him try to convince people to view God his way."

"You know what helps me?" she said. "I think of my husband as Jesus when he's in the pulpit. Jesus giving me a message each week."

I sighed. If I had wanted to marry Jesus, thought the Bitch, I would have become a nun.

As Chuck established the new church, I did my best to find a place in the twilight zone of robes and bread and grape juice. I taught adult Sunday school classes and even gave an occasional sermon on spirituality and creativity.

Meanwhile, I fought with Chuck about the evening meetings he often forgot to forecast. "What makes your work take automatic priority tonight? I brought work home. How am I going to get it done, plus help Jess with his library research, plus give Keeg a ride to soccer?"

"Can you do your work before I leave?" Chuck asked. "I can make dinner."

"It's always about your schedule, isn't it?"

"I'm sorry that it's a busy week."

"It's not just about this week. You've chosen a busy life."

"Suz—"

"It's like you're having an affair with the church while your marriage is falling apart. And the boys are growing up while Reverend Wonderful is spending his life at church."

I jogged. I went into therapy, climbing the creaking stairs of an old, two-story house near downtown Iowa City, sitting on a couch, and placing the Bitch on the table for dissection, trying to understand the hateful shrew inside. Howard, the psychologist, sat in an overstuffed chair, listening like a benevolent older brother.

"You and Chuck started dating at what age?"

"Fifteen."

Howard stroked his beard. "You knew each other at such a young age that maybe your personalities became intermingled. You might be at a sorting-out place, needing to discover your own self. You might actually be a mystery to yourself."

I stared out the window. "I do know that I don't like to go to church. I never have."

I told him about the chastising sermons of my youth and my realization in high school that I was an atheist, then later realizing I was more of an agnostic.

I told him about preferring to spend my Sunday mornings outdoors. "It's much more rejuvenating to take a walk in the woods than listen to my husband preach."

"Have you thought about not going?"

Silence.

He spoke again. "When you find that you don't like

purple shirts, doesn't there come a time when you just have to acknowledge that you don't like purple shirts?"

"I have thought about not going," I said slowly, "but I worry about the damage to Chuck's image. I think the congregation would think I wasn't being supportive."

"Why do you care? Why do you suppose you're so self-conscious?"

"He was told by his supervisor last year that I would ruin his career if I don't participate. And when we lived in Iowa Falls, especially after I was an adult, I often heard older women complain about ministers' wives. They weren't active enough in the women's circles, their hair looked awful, their kids weren't well-behaved, they were sick too often. Recently a woman married to a retired minister told me that when her kids got into school, she wanted to go back to teaching but had to ask the congregation's permission. They told her, 'You can work if you still teach Sunday school and play piano during the service.'"

"Did she?"

I nodded. "She told me that to 'show them,' she 'did it all.' She seemed so proud of herself." I sighed. "Martyrdom isn't the answer for me. I just don't want to be so angry so often. All Chuck can talk and think about is his work. Everybody reinforces him; nobody seems the least concerned about my feelings."

"Maybe these intense emotions you have when he receives the attention are an act of love or sacrifice on your part," Howard mused. "Maybe you've been assigned the role of critic in your marriage. The payoff for Chuck might be that you help keep his ego in line. But what's your payoff?"

Anger as an act of love. It seemed preposterous. "I don't know. I guess lashing out just helps diminish the anger, at least for a little while. But then I feel like such a bitch."

"Rather than focusing on that, think about the cost it incurs to you. The cost in self-dignity."

Tearing up, I reached for a Kleenex on the lamp stand. "But how do I change these dynamics?"

"Very slowly, most likely. By realizing they'll occur again. By having a plan. By knowing that even small changes can produce confusion and anger in other areas."

I visualized an arcade game that Jess and Keegan liked to play at Chuckie Cheese. Rubber, faux-haired moles popped up from below a tabletop. The object was to get all the moles pounded down with a wooden mallet, but the more creatures they hit, the faster other moles sprung up. The Bitch was like the moles: she was everywhere, ever ready.

One early winter Saturday morning at 6:00, Keegan and I delivered the boys' newspaper route, letting Jesse sleep. Chuck and I alternated this way with the boys on Saturdays. Rain the night before had turned to several inches of snow—wet and heavy, sticky and beautiful, soft, insulating, quiet. But after walking several blocks, we heard a homeowner pushing his noisy snowblower down his driveway.

We are all so busy, I thought, making our nests, not noticing the grace and beauty before us. I thought about the way the character Shug muses in Alice Walker's *The Color Purple*, "I think it pisses God off if you walk by the color purple in a field somewhere and don't notice it." But I identified with the operator of the snowblower, except my noise was internal. Inside, I was busy and noisily emoting and resenting.

Papers delivered, eight-year-old Keegan and I walked home side by side. Catching a fat snowflake in my mouth, I gave my son a tight hug and he leaned sleepily into me. "Shall I make some hot chocolate?"

"Yeah," he said, his voice husky, "and then I might go back to bed."

I vowed that morning to relax a little. My conversations with Howard weren't providing instant results, but they were at least helping me accept the Bitch—the mother dog protecting her vulnerable pup—i.e., me—until my legs were firm, until I knew who I was and could make my own boundaries, not let others set them for me.

"Some revolutionaries immediately go out into the street to make changes," Howard told me. "Others are forced into the street by their own logic. I think you're one of the latter."

I nodded. "All along, I've looked for a mentor. I thought if I knew just one minister's wife who walked her own path, I could cope. Maybe I have to be my own mentor. And maybe I'll be one for someone else down the line."

Understanding and letting the Bitch guide me wasn't a linear process. It was more like wandering into a maze and sometimes finding my way out, other times getting caught in a corner or a loop. Why did I keep re-entering? Because I wanted our family to continue having meals together around the table every evening. Yes, I wanted to keep going. Trying to learn from the Bitch was the only way I knew how.

One evening in December, Chuck and I attended the Christmas holiday meal for the district clergy at Cornell College in Mount Vernon. Two hundred clergy and spouses sat around cloth-covered, circular tables in a dining room. Before dinner there were speeches and jokes, a scripture reading, and a short sermon by the district superintendent. At our table, a pastor made irreverent, *sotto voce* comments in between the speeches, trying to elicit chuckles.

I didn't think his jokes were all that funny, but I tolerated the comic, folded my hands, and kept my head down during the prayer. Then, while college students in white shirts and black slacks served the dinner, I turned to the quiet, middle-aged woman next to me who was married to the jokester.

"Where do you two live?" I asked politely.

She looked me over. "What do you care?" she said. Out of the corner of my eye I saw her husband lean to the pastor on his left and, oblivious to his wife glaring at me, make another clever comment.

I smiled.

God bless us both, I thought. Bitch-selves and all.

CHAPTER 5

Callings

1990–93

WHILE CHUCK EMBRACED HIS NEW VOCATION, I STRUGGLED with increasing boredom as a test editor at ACT.

Every day during the allotted half-hour lunch, I walked two miles with other editors from my department. Blinking in the sun after our morning in the windowless basement, we joked about work tedium or shared dreams about being independently wealthy enough so we could write, draw, or make music. We all craved time to be creative.

One warm day in May, I broke ahead of the group and caught up with Julie, a statistician several steps up on the pay and status hierarchy. For several days I'd noticed her walking alone. "Hey, Julie, if you ever want to join us, we usually walk during this time," I said, gesturing to the group.

She removed a pair of earphones and smiled but shook her head. "Thanks, but I really enjoy this. Listen." She handed me the earphones.

I expected lively music but heard the sharp, even click of a metronome set at allegro. Julie looked at me expectantly.

"I can vary the beat," she said. "If I want to get my heart rate up, I set it faster, and when I want to cool down, I just slow the beat."

I thought about the B.B. King, Van Morrison, and Gloria Estefan tunes I listened to on my Walkman whenever I could find time to jog around our neighborhood: the bossy bass of "Why I Sing the Blues," the twirling rhythm of "Cuts Both Ways." Suddenly I could see my boredom philosophically at ACT: I simply didn't fit the clinical, measured culture. The longer I stayed, the more cynical I would probably become.

Julie retrieved her headphones from my hand. "Thanks anyway, Sue. See you later. I don't want my heart rate to slow down yet!"

I longed for fulfilling work. I wanted to teach English at a community college. I taught night classes as an adjunct at Kirkwood Community College, a half-hour away in Cedar Rapids. I'd interviewed for several full-time positions but had been turned down two years in a row. Now, in mid-June, after a long silence following my third interview, I assumed that my third application had gone nowhere.

One day after work I drove to the woods along the Coralville Reservoir and hiked to a rocky cliff overlooking the water. I stared down at the waves lapping the shore. Why wasn't teaching in the cards for me, I wondered. Why was Chuck able to pursue his dream but I wasn't? We'd lived in Iowa Falls for an entire decade so he could help run his dad's business, and now here he was, doing ministry.

When would it be my turn?

I marched for a mile along a path close to the shore. As I turned back toward the parking lot, my mind finally empty, a quiet but strong thought (from my intuition?) arose: "Support Chuck. Trust that it will work. You, too, will find your calling." Numb but peaceful, I climbed back into the car and headed home.

A month later, in mid-July, I accepted an offer to teach writing and literature full-time at Kirkwood.

"Hey, you pricks! Hey, Sue!" Ed sauntered in, saluting a few early classmates and me on the second day of Composition I class during my fourth fall of teaching at Kirkwood. Ed had said a few inappropriate things the first day of class, too, but instead of confronting him I distracted him as I would a toddler until I knew him better. By the end of that first hour, I decided he meant well but needed some basic training in classroom etiquette.

I surveyed the classroom. Just a few early students, so I wouldn't embarrass Ed in front of the entire class if I said something. Students take their dignity seriously even when they act undignified. "Ed," I said, with as genuine a smile as I could muster, "Please call me Suzanne. And I'm sure your classmates would rather be called something besides 'pricks.'"

"Sure thing, Teach—Sue—Suzanne," replied Ed, smiling back. He walked over to me, his six-foot-six frame towering over my own five feet. "Sure wish you'd grow a little, though." The other students snickered.

"If I grew, who would you make jokes about?"

"Better just take vitamins, Teach." Ed patted my shoulder and ambled toward a desk too small for his body.

I would be surprised to learn that Ed had served two years in the Army. He hated the experience so much he wouldn't talk about it in class, though he freely advertised his weekend party plans, often inviting me to "Stop by for a beer, Teach."

Then there was Cindy, a brash young mother who told the class she had been diagnosed with fetal alcohol syndrome after her mother abandoned her. Whenever I entered the room before class, Cindy leaned forward in her chair in the front row, her slender form ready to pounce. "This essay is hard to write," she might say, her voice accusing. Or "I hated this reading." Or "My baby girl kept me awake all night, so I'm drinking this Coke to stay awake." She reminded us of her baby as often as Pat, in the back row, rubbed the tattoos on his forearm.

The whispering ones were a challenge too. Several young women at the back talked to each other during class discussions. I talked to the whisperers privately after the third class. "Do you know each other from other classes?"

"Yes, we went to high school together," one volunteered.

"Great. But please keep your social conversations out of the room. I need you to pay attention. We're laying groundwork for an essay you'll be writing."

John, a young man of solid build who wore a black stocking hat, added the class two weeks late, against my better judgment. He'd offered what sounded like a reasonable excuse. I finally said, "Okay, you're in, but you cannot afford to miss anymore class days for the rest of the semester." He'd nodded, silent, with a pleasant smile revealing even, white teeth. Two weeks later he skipped. When he returned the next time, I asked him to stay after class. "John, you seem as if you don't want to be here. You don't say a word and don't even seem to pay attention to your classmates when they talk.

Please either attend and join the community or drop the class." He never missed again. He rarely uttered a word, but his writing began to show an endearingly skeptical, sensitive bent, even though riddled with the errors of an unpracticed or dyslexic reader.

Overall, these freshman composition students were among the least mature students I'd had. I began the semester with difficult essays that I hoped would spark good discussions. I asked them to write summaries of the readings but instead received personal, stream-of-consciousness responses: "I don't think this guy knows what he's talking about because he's writing way over my head." Their mechanical errors were terrible: improper capitalizations, run-on sentences, comma splices, and bad grammar. I was disheartened, but I knew I needed to teach them how to be students—how to carefully read difficult texts, reflect on their reading, and write with confidence.

The fifth week we discussed Plato's "Allegory of the Cave."

"I get it!" Cindy yelled, her thin frame rocketing out of the seat. "This guy is saying that most of us want to sit in the cave!"

"Yeah," said one of the former whisperers as her friends nodded. "And when people come out into the light—if they do, and lots of people don't—they're blinded."

"And so then they want to go back into their cave, which is at least familiar, even though it's dark and full of illusion," Pat said, stroking his tattoos.

"Oh yeah, man," Ed intoned from the back row. "I guess you have to get used to the light. If you lose your illusions, it takes a while for reality to come clear. Kind of like being here in school. You hate somebody trying to teach you something, but once in a while, it clicks."

I smiled. "Very impressive." Even quiet John smiled, his white teeth lighting up his face.

In and around my busy teaching life, I continued to read articles and books by Christian theologians in my ongoing effort to understand and support Chuck's attraction to ministry. I read books by Christian feminists Elisabeth Schüssler Fiorenza and Phyllis Trible and researched theological interpretations of the

Original Bitch: Eve. I shared the research in my Introduction to Literature class, where students crowded three times a week into a temporary classroom on the edge of campus.

"What do you know about Eve in the Garden of Eden story from the Judeo-Christian tradition?" I asked thirty-five freshmen and sophomores. "We're going to look at it from a literary standpoint."

"She ate the apple and then tempted Adam to eat one too."

"She introduced sin and death into the world."

"She's evil; she's the reason women are second-class citizens."

"Where did you get these impressions?" I asked.

Bill grinned slyly from the back row. "Comic books, cartoons."

"So, Temptress, Evil Agent of Sin, Second-class Citizen. Are there other ways we can look at Eve? Maybe more neutral or even positive ways?"

"She could be seen as gullible," said one student.

"Or helpless," another said.

"Or thoughtful, curious. A risk-taker," said Alissa, a front-row feminist.

"What is the story really about?" I asked.

"It's the story of humans who slipped from bliss to sin," said a somber student in the middle row. "It's about the consequences of disobedience."

"No, it's about how boring life would be if things were perfect" came from the back.

"It's about the importance of knowledge."

"Really, it's about coming into consciousness. It's about a loss of innocence, and it's part of being alive. You have to experience it," said Rob.

I told the students about how Jewish and Christian leaders had interpreted the Garden of Eden over the centuries. "The command God gave Adam and Eve to be fruitful and multiply was used to justify the Jewish emphasis on marriage and family. But then some early Christian preachers advocated 'undoing the sin of Adam and Eve' by choosing celibacy."

"Kind of contradictory, isn't it?" asked one student.

I nodded. "In the Middle Ages, Eve was associated with witchcraft. In 1486 the Dominicans wrote, 'All witchcraft comes from carnal lust, which in women is insatiable.' Eve was seen as more closely related to Satan than Adam, capable of exercising a demonic power over her husband."

"Way to go, baby," cried Alissa, pumping her arm in the air.

"Some say this interpretation of Eve is what prompted the Jewish custom of women wearing head coverings; because of Eve's sin, women going bare-headed was considered similar to exposing a physical deformity."

Alissa made a thumbs-down sign.

"The Garden of Eden story was used politically, too, to keep people under Roman authority from questioning the Roman rule."

"Are there other interpretations of this story?" someone asked.

I smiled and took a breath in the musty room, the carpet stained by a leaky ceiling in the "temporary" classroom that felt like a large mobile home and had been on campus forty years. The college had grown so quickly that new construction couldn't keep up with enrollment.

"Some of the early Christians—the Gnostics—read the story as a myth about our loss of contact with God and a fall into ordinary consciousness, like Rob suggested. Some even saw Eve as the enlightened one who awakened Adam into awareness of his spiritual nature."

Alissa pumped her fist again.

"During the Age of Enlightenment in the seventeenth and eighteenth centuries, the story was seen by some as a rise, not a fall, a transition from infancy to adulthood, from ignorance to mature human knowledge. Feminists see Eve as a hero—someone who takes risks. I also like to turn the story in on itself and look at it as a story about the nature of story. It teaches what makes good, rich stories: not moralistic messages, but stories with conflict and complex layers of meaning. We could think of Eve as the Mother of Stories."

I looked at my students. Most seemed engaged; a few at the back looked sleepy this midafternoon. I thought about the courage our mythical Eve displayed. Call her a witch, a temptress, a bitch—but in my book, she was a hero because, above all, she wanted to live authentically. She wanted to use all her faculties. She wanted to know. She traded a simple life of ignorance and dependence for a life rich in complexity and conflict. Isn't that our responsibility in life—to be who we are, to live, to embrace the journey, even when it is difficult?

"Let's turn to 'Young Goodman Brown.' The class groaned as we shifted from the short, spare Garden of Eden piece to

Hawthorne's dense classic, but they opened their books. "I think you'll see echoes of the Garden of Eden story."

During finals week that year, Ed poked his head in my office door. He had taken to stopping by frequently for brief help sessions, always leaving with a pat on the shoulder and a "Grow up, will ya?" I skimmed the rough draft of his final essay and made suggestions. "Ed, your writing has really improved. Do you realize that?" For the first time, he hung his head, shy, but he nodded. As he left, I relished what would be his last pat for the semester.

Soon, quiet John slipped in and proudly waved his portfolio, a collection of his semester's writing. It was late. He flashed a smile, which I returned. "Thank you, John, and I'll have it for you when we meet on Friday." He bowed humorously as he backed out of the office. I put his portfolio on the bottom of the pile.

Finally, at the end of the last day of finals week, I opened John's portfolio. Along with his semester's writing, he had included a letter to me, free of errors and elegantly written. He told about years of drug addiction, attempts to get clean, a bad car accident, and a few self-sabotaging attempts to go back to school while taking advantage of "loopholes" and excuses. "Only one of my professors took notice," he wrote. "I remember vividly what you said when I was caught and started to turn on the ignorance. 'You seem as if you don't want to be in class.' Wow. I hadn't been slapped back like that in years." He shaped himself up after that, he wrote. "I would like to send out a heartfelt thank you to the professor who taught me that it is better to try than to hold on for the ride."

On this day during finals week, I felt I was exactly where I needed to be, doing what I needed to do. Yes, my teaching load was crushing, with five classes and 120–140 students per semester. Yes, I wished I had more time for my family, not to mention for myself.

But that small, reassuring voice (my intuition? the divine? both?) that had said, "Support Chuck. Trust that it will work. You, too, will find your calling"—it hadn't lied.

I sat back in my chair. Chuck's decision to be a minister had not made my life a dead end after all. Chuck touched people's lives. And so did I.

At thirty-eight, I was feeling the magic of our hectic lives as spouses and parents, teacher and preacher.

CHAPTER 6

Suspension of Disbelief

1994

IT WASN'T THE MESSAGE SO MUCH AS THE MESSENGER. AFTER all, I'd known him first as that wise-cracking fifth-grade drummer who held his drumsticks like devil's horns behind the serious Stephanie as she kept perfect rhythm with her bass drum. Little did any of us know that the boy to whom the band director often shouted, "Settle down, Kelsey," would someday be a preacher.

Nor did I suspect that one day I would have to try to take him seriously, this man who hiked his underwear to just below his chest, puffed out his stomach, bared his teeth like a horse, and dove into bed at night, so pleased when I laughed. When I listened to Chuck preach, I had to rid myself of those slapstick images. Then I had to ignore the weird facial expressions he made in the pulpit—the exaggerated smiles that turned down at the corner to hide dimples, the thick eyebrows raised for emphasis.

Literature suspends our disbelief in serpents that talk or people who grow wings. But I struggled to suspend my disbelief listening to Chuck's sermons.

Occasionally, though, they drew me in. Like the time he began by reminiscing about his fifth-grade year, a memory that had been triggered the week before as he listened to Nancy Sinatra's "These Boots Are Made for Walking" on the radio. His parents had a fifty-cow milking operation then. For two years, Chuck arose at 4:30 a.m., rain or snow, for morning milking. Each day after school he would eat, milk again, do schoolwork, and go to bed early. The days began and ended with the cows.

A fifth-grade teacher occasionally thumped students on their ears for talking out of turn. "One day I received her thump," Chuck said, "and I became very discouraged." The weight of the world was on his overworked shoulders. "Fifth grade was a time of feeling king of the school one day and the next getting chosen last for kickball. And then there was the daily milking routine. Fifth grade was hard," he said, seriously. "It was very hard."

He paused long enough for the congregation to recall their own preadolescent years. Mine, too, were difficult—my ugly duckling years. I needed braces for two nearly horizontal front teeth and a severe overbite. I rarely smiled, and when I did, I certainly didn't let my teeth show. In two years, my parents would scrape together the money for braces, but I knew nothing of that in fifth grade. I wore "Chubette" clothes, as they were called, and felt left out as I watched my best friend blossom, making new friends.

Yes, Chuck, I agreed. Fifth grade was hard. A tear rolled down my cheek as I empathized. My stoic husband so rarely admitted that anything was difficult—a habit born, I was sure, in those years of milking. When he did, you knew it was tough. Our sons' daily afternoon paper route and early Saturday morning deliveries were nothing by comparison.

"But the song playing in the milk parlor, as Mom and I relieved the cows of their daily offerings, helped me. It comforted me. The phrase 'These boots are made for walking' reminded me that I wasn't the only one going through a tough time. Somehow that made me feel better."

As I sat in the pew, I remembered Sinatra wearing white go-go boots when she sang that song in the sixties. I'd longed for a pair, certain they would help me overcome my shyness, but I dared not ask my hard-working parents.

Chuck continued, "But most comforting of all that year were my Mom and Dad, who reassured me that I was needed. I was special, I knew, as we sat in the barn together and milked those cows. They never said as much. I just knew from their presence."

Chuck drew an analogy between his parents' love and God's unconditional love, but I stayed with the image of his parents. His mother would have been in her mid-thirties, a little younger than Chuck and me, his father ten years older. I imagined her wearing a plaid car coat, a wool scarf tied below her chin. I saw his father with dark hair, not yet gray, silently tethering the cows for Chuck and his mother to milk by hand. I could hear cows moo, could smell their manure, and see it steaming in winter. I pictured a few cats sitting on the backs of the Holsteins, meowing for squirts of milk.

I had no doubt that Chuck's parents offered him that gift of reassurance and acceptance. They had that grace about them. Their door was always open, coffee always ready to pour, food plentiful even when money was not. They had an unusual ability to wordlessly comfort those around them and had passed that quality onto their son.

While Chuck's parents had the support of his father's parents on the family farm, mine struggled without parents nearby, each working full-time yet finding time to nurture my brother, sister, and me. They knew our differences and supported each of us where it counted—my sister as a naturalist and creative seamstress; my brother as a comic, athlete, and future CPA; me as a clarinetist and dreaming writer/artist. Despite their work schedules, Mom and Dad conveyed that we were special and needed. They continued to offer loving support to us and their six grandchildren.

"Rejoice with me," Chuck said at the end of his sermon, referring to a passage in Luke 15. "Rejoice with me; I have found my lost sheep" (15:6), says a shepherd. And "Rejoice with me; I have found my lost coin" (15:9), says a woman. Chuck reminded us that though we feel lost at times, as he did in fifth grade, there is rejoicing when we know we are accepted by those we love—and by God.

I did rejoice with him that Sunday. I surrendered my disbelief to him. I watched not his down-turned lips; I noticed not his rumpled suit; I recalled not the argument we'd had the week before, nor the silly dive he made into bed after we reconciled. I did rejoice with him—in the way divine energy created him and me and our sons and our parents and his grandmother and our siblings and the congregation and our neighbors and our growing community of friends and the flame red maple tree we planted in front of our duplex that weekend. In all things, mundane and sublime, I rejoiced. With him.

CHAPTER 7

Sharing the Robe

1995

IT WAS ELEVEN THIRTY, AND CHUCK AND I WERE AWAKE AND amorous. In the middle of our passion, the phone rang. We froze. Chuck finally grabbed the phone from the bedroom desk; calls after bedtime were usually emergencies. I heard Joan's voice from across the room, unbuffered by his ear, which was a few inches away from the receiver. She talked at length, Chuck finally breaking in: "That's okay, the meeting will still roll without him; we'll just get someone else to give the report." He dropped his voice, signaling closure, but Joan didn't get it. He listened awhile, then said, "Yes," with more emphasis. Again, she missed her cue. Finally, he said, "Can I call you tomorrow to discuss this? I was in a deep sleep." He grinned and rolled his eyes at me.

Other women's needs surfaced. Cheryl had lunch with Chuck to discuss problems with her boss. Jenny needed chemotherapy; Chuck drove her to the hospital because her husband was unavailable. I knew they needed help and chided myself for resenting them as they helped themselves to pieces of my husband.

I found no mentors, no role models, no confidantes in other ministers' spouses about this issue of sharing one's mate. There seemed to be some unspoken code against complaint. Years earlier, when Chuck was a lay youth leader in our hometown Methodist church, I had a conversation with the head minister's wife. She and I sat in the parsonage backyard after a barbeque. "Kathy, how do you deal with being married to a minister?" I asked. "Do you find it strange to share your husband? To live such a public life?"

Her permed hair glowed in the sun as she shook her head with an emphatic "No." She and her husband, Stephen, both in their late thirties, had been married only a year; it was her first marriage, his second. His children stayed with them every other weekend; their enthusiastic shouts from inside the house mingled with those of our sons. "Stephen is the best thing that has ever happened to me," she said. "I'm just grateful to be with him. I like it here."

Older women in the congregation grumbled about Kathy not joining the women's circles, but she sang in the choir, flashing her beautiful smile at the congregation. She also seemed to keep her own life intact, taking classes at the community college and enjoying her own interests. Several years after we moved away, I heard Stephen had an affair with a parishioner, Kathy divorced him, and she suffered from depression. Eventually, Stephen married a third wife.

As my forties loomed, I learned that three ministers in the Iowa conference left their middle-aged wives for younger parishioners within a few months of one another. One clergy spouse I knew had frequent migraine headaches; one divorced her husband after too many years of feeling like a single parent of three children; one, a minister herself, divorced her clergy husband; three others besides Kathy suffered from chronic depression; and one, after twenty-odd years, convinced her husband to exit the ministry. Out of the dozen ministers' wives I knew, only one or two seemed to have the inner peace about which their husbands preached regularly.

I knew the rational, Dear Abby thing to do was take other women's interest in Chuck as reinforcement for my choice in a great mate. Instead, I struggled silently, too ashamed to admit my dirty little secret: I didn't like sharing my husband.

One Sunday morning I sat down in the church sanctuary with a sigh, patting myself on the back for getting the family to church. While Jess read a novel during Chuck's sermon, Keegan kicked his legs. I whispered, "Stop swinging." He asked for a piece of gum. I smiled at him and dug into my pocket, producing gum for him and a piece for Jess, who accepted it without looking up from his book. The Sunday before, when Chuck glanced our way, we subtly pantomimed flicking lighters, rock band groupie style. Subversive parishioners.

After the sermon I breathed a sigh of relief. The sermon seemed well-developed; the English teacher in me couldn't help noticing. I didn't disagree with anything he said. He didn't stretch his mouth that weird way he sometimes did when he preached. Maybe he was growing into this role after all. Maybe I was just getting more used to it. Probably both. Relief filled me with a floating feeling of benevolence.

After the benediction I rose, and the boys rushed ahead past the receiving line to grab donuts. I saw June, a slender, well-dressed widow in her late seventies, give Chuck a full frontal embrace, her arms around his neck like a lover. Body slam! Chuck patted her shoulder gingerly but backed up. He took her hands from his neck and held them in front to create a distance between their bodies.

I drew closer to Chuck to offer a smirk. But now standing in front of him was another woman, this one my age, about forty. Her hair was shoulder length and parted in the middle. She was slender and beautiful in a frail, manicured way—hair curled, fingernails painted. One red-tipped finger was fondling the pewter peace symbol Chuck wore on the lapel of his suit. Chuck had mentioned her stopping by his office a few times for counseling. Now I wondered: Was she seeking an emotional affair with him to provide relief from—what? An inattentive husband? A boring life? I was as shocked by her graceful finger on my husband's jacket as if I had seen her standing naked before him. Chuck also seemed taken aback. Once again, I watched him take a quick step back to signal a more professional distance.

I turned away from this intimate moment I wished I hadn't seen, put on my coat, and ushered the boys home.

And so I wrestled with sharing my husband. I also continued to struggle at seeing him in a minister's robe. Whether the traditional black flowing style or the off-white monk's alb, the robe accentuated his public persona, which seemed so different from the Chuck I'd known so many years.

There were intellectual and historical grounds for my aversion. I'd read that this type of garb was officially adopted by clergy centuries after Christ, at about the same time the church cut women out of the leadership roles they'd held during Christ's lifetime and for several centuries after. By the fourteenth century, when secular men favored pants, clergy in western Europe were setting themselves apart with long gowns. During this time, the church sanctioned the torture and killing of at least thirty thousand and possibly up to nine million other wearers of long gowns: women they labeled witches.

An ex-minister friend, Bob, shared his "feminization of the clergy" theory: He felt that women subtly encourage male ministers to hide their masculinity by adopting a more feminine, caring persona. Hiding the maleness under a robe allows women to safely gather around this atypical male creature whose job it is to be interested in their well-being. Bob resented the demasculinization, citing it as one reason for leaving the ministry.

On one hand, his theory helped me see the robe's value in suppressing the erotic component to a pastor's relationship with parishioners. On the other hand, it reinforced the idea that as a minister, Chuck was putting himself up for grabs by those in need. And those in need, or at least those who pursued help, tended to be women more often than men.

We were at a party. Two older women walked up to me after meeting Chuck for the first time. "I think your husband is just wonderful," the eighty-year-old said to me, giggling.

Instantly I felt rebellious, but I smiled and blithely said, "Oh, women always love Chuck."

"Well, of course!" said the sixty-five-year-old woman with beautiful, thick gray hair. "He's a minister!"

She was an itinerant artist, barely scraping by. She stopped by the church now and then to ask for money. She was a little older than me, but a rough life and too much sun and cigarettes had added years to her face.

I'd seen her three times: twice after church as she slipped in to ask for gas money, once downtown as she told Chuck about her next painting project. All three times she stood awfully close to Chuck; each time he backed up a step. The day we saw her downtown, she kept her blue eyes on him. Like a smitten lover, she told him about her plans, her needs, her project.

I might have liked her; we had a love of art in common. But the way she only had eyes for Chuck held me at bay. She seemed reluctant, or unwilling, to acknowledge my presence. All three times, after telling her part and Chuck finally interrupting her to introduce me, she smiled briefly at me, her eyes cold or insecure, and left immediately. As she walked away, I noticed that her shorts didn't quite cover her bottom.

Even after decades of feminism, some women were still looking for the magical prince-pastor who would take care of them.

Or was it just that I wanted my own prince to myself?

I couldn't control the occasional times when another woman might have more eros than agape on her mind. I also couldn't control my husband's actions or reactions. I knew this was mostly about my learning to give up control—to let go and trust Chuck to make his boundaries clear. I also knew that if I didn't get it this time, the opportunity to improve at sharing the robe would surely circle around again and again. And again.

CHAPTER 8

Rejoice, Request, Relax

1996

WHEN I HEARD CHUCK'S SERMON ONE SUNDAY BEFORE
Christmas, I was not intrigued. He suggested we keep the three
Rs in mind as we approached Christmas: rejoice, request, relax.
"Rejoice in Christ's coming," he said authoritatively, his fingers
gripping the lectern, "make our requests known to God, and
relax and enjoy."

Of course, I thought. Common sense. Ho hum. Glancing
around the congregation, I wondered if others shared my lack of
enthusiasm. I saw thoughtful looks and nodding heads. At least
the message resonated with some.

Two nights later, I desperately tried to recall the three Rs.
Unable to sleep, I quietly left Chuck's deep breathing, closed the
bedroom door, descended to the living room of our little duplex,
and plugged in the Christmas tree lights. Wrapping myself in
a colorful log cabin quilt made by Chuck's Grandma Cord, I
sighed and sat on the futon in front of the tree. I turned things
over in my mind while my eyes traced the opaque lights of pink,
red, blue, green, white, and yellow.

It was five days before Christmas, but Chuck and I still
hadn't decided what to give Jess, sixteen, and Keegan, twelve.
Every year I had that tug of war between two impulses: trying
to escape the commercialism of the season, yet wanting to give
our sons the perfect gift, no matter the cost. Part of me wanted
to let our sons know, in a material way, just how much they had
enriched our lives, given us countless moments to savor, given
me a sense of purpose. They made me feel needed. They had

taught patience and given joy. Every year, though, I kept the lid on my impulse to be extravagant, settling for moderately priced gifts that left them politely grateful.

This year we had ideas that might actually please and surprise them, if only we had the courage. To be more precise, if only I did; Chuck was waiting for me to decide. But the difference between courage and stupidity can be slight. For three hours, five nights before Christmas, I pondered that difference.

Keegan had long wanted a dog. He had begged, pleaded—his blue eyes piercing, expressive eyebrows raised almost in pain—for a dog.

"But we're gone too much of the day," I would say.

"I'll walk it before and after school every day," he would counter, shifting from foot to foot.

"But you're often busy after school."

"I'll walk it as soon as I get home."

"Dogs need lots of space. We don't have a big yard."

"Our dog will get the most exercise of any dog in the neighborhood. You like to walk, so sometimes you'd walk it. And Jesse and Dad would too."

For three years I'd scanned the classifieds for dogs, looking for an already grown and trained pet. When Chuck and I discussed the subject privately, I played Keegan's role. "The boys really need a pet," I would say.

"So let's get them a guinea pig."

"But think of all the animals you had on the farm when you were a kid: cows, pigs, indoor and outdoor cats, a couple of dogs for best friends. You don't realize how much of a delight a pet can be for a city kid. When Mom and Dad gave us Schautzie, I was overjoyed, and I loved that dog all those years! You take animals for granted."

On the Monday night before Christmas, I dreamed that a stranger dropped off at our duplex a short-haired, tan puppy with a dark brown muzzle. Inspecting its paws, we decided it wouldn't grow too big and welcomed it into our family. There was a sensation of sailing as we held the puppy. Music played, like an ending to a happy movie. I laughed as I told Chuck about the dream the next morning.

Over coffee we decided to check the animal shelter for suitable pets. Waiting outside with a half-dozen people for the shelter to open, we noticed a young blonde woman crying softly. A puppy with a dark brown muzzle poked its nose out of her coat. I froze, waiting to see the color of the dog's body. After admitting everyone to the building, the clerk began to ask the woman questions about the puppy. She pulled the creature out of her coat; its fur was tan. We listened intently to the conversation.

"She's a mixed breed. The vet speculated some Elkhound, or Keeshond, or Chow, maybe some German Shepherd. She's eight weeks old."

"Yes, she's had her first round of shots."

"I can't keep her because it's against the rules to have dogs in my apartment. I took her without thinking it through. I can't keep hiding her from the landlord. She doesn't bark much, but when she does, I'm afraid I'll be kicked out."

Chuck and I moved closer and asked, "What kind of temperament does she have? Is she house-broken?"

Through tears, the woman responded. "She's a good puppy in every way. Very sweet. No accidents. Sleeps all night in her kennel. I wouldn't give her up if I didn't have to."

The clerk tilted her head sympathetically. "Listen, folks, if you're interested in taking this puppy, you'd better have this conversation outside. It will be cheaper for all of you if we aren't involved. We have procedures to follow, like waiting periods and fees."

Outside, the young woman repeated her praise. The dog sat quietly but alert in her arms. The same size and shape as the puppy in my dream the night before, she had soft, silky fur.

"What do you call her?" I asked.

"Lucy."

I whispered to Chuck. "This is the same puppy I had in my dream." He nodded, remembering the description I'd given him that morning.

The girl offered the puppy for Chuck to hold. "I'll step away so you can talk this over."

Chuck gently petted the creature. It looked good in his arms. "Let's take it," he said. The skeptic had melted.

Which stole my confidence. What were we doing? "You know, maybe we shouldn't take it right now—it's too impulsive. We've talked about an adult pet, not a puppy. I only have two more weeks until school starts again. I don't know if we have the time and patience to train a puppy. We need to separate our decision from this girl's distress."

"But it will cost her and us more that way. It's cute; its temperament seems gentle but not fearful. Let's just take it."

"We're talking about a puppy that needs training, and we're not prepared for that. How about we ask her to check it in and think about this overnight."

Slowly, we handed the puppy back to the young woman, whose tears resumed. I said, "We're really excited about her, but we need more time to think it over. If you'll give me your name and number, I'll let you know what we decide."

Later that afternoon I discovered Chuck had a card up his sleeve. He wanted to negotiate. "You know what would please Jess just as much as a puppy would Keeg?" he began. "We could bring the Nova out of storage and fix it up for him. I've checked on prices for the engine repair. It's not as expensive as we thought."

Jess, sixteen, had had his driver's license for five months and had been asking for his own car. He shaved now, and his face was angular, his voice deep. But I was reluctant to provide him with his own car. Why be a three-car family if we could limp along with two? With careful planning and the occasional help of friends, we'd get by.

Eight years earlier we bought the Chevy Nova new so I could have a reliable car for commuting to graduate school. Shiny silver with a dressy red stripe down each side, the car made me feel invincible as I drove the hour each way from our home in Iowa Falls to Iowa State University in Ames. Now a little rusty, the car was still a symbol to me of our escape from our hometown. For several years Jess had teasingly claimed it for himself, but I'd secretly been relieved when the car broke down shortly before his sixteenth birthday. Even with engine work, the mechanics warned us they didn't know how many miles it would continue. We'd decided to store the car. Jess had accepted this decision stoically, as was his nature.

"I don't know if I'm ready for him to have his own car," I told Chuck. "And we've gotten along pretty well with just two."

"Only because I've run myself ragged making sure everyone has transportation when they need it," Chuck said.

I reluctantly agreed. "While I'm teaching, you probably do more running than I realize."

That Tuesday night as I curled up in front of the Christmas tree, I probed each of the decisions. What if the puppy wasn't trainable, or couldn't cope with being alone four or five hours during the day, or didn't take to us? What if she got much bigger than expected?

And Jesse. What had happened to that little boy who hunted for tadpoles in a creek that fed the Iowa River?

The Nova was small. Would it leave him vulnerable in an accident? Would he be tempted to drive too fast since it zipped along so easily? Could we afford to maintain three cars, especially if I was already fantasizing about cutting to part-time teaching after only six years full-time?

As I named the worries, my body tensed. Then I thought back to Chuck's sermon a few days earlier. "Rejoice, request, relax," he had said, so sure of himself. Okay, Rev, I thought. I'll put your formula to work. This obsessing is getting me nowhere.

Rejoice. What did I have to rejoice about? That was easy. Plenty. The beauty of the tree lights. The coziness of the living room. The little duplex—small, but still twice the size of our old apartment. That we could afford Christmas without debt. Family. The boys. Chuck. That my parents had retired and done some traveling. My siblings and their families. Chuck's siblings and parents. That I was on break for a couple more weeks. That we had regular Friday night pizza and spontaneous walks in the woods with a widening circle of friends.

Having a husband whose faith in God was so quiet and strong without being pushy. Being graced with a faith myself after twenty-odd years of skepticism. It wasn't a faith that lent itself to organized religion, but it was still a faith in a divine something-or-other.

Yes, I had much to rejoice about.

Request. How could one make requests without being greedy? What business did I have asking for anything I didn't already have?

But Chuck had said it so confidently.

I was wavering under the juggling act of balancing our two strenuous careers with raising our sons. Arlie Hochschild called it "the time bind" in her book *The Time Bind: When Work Becomes Home and Home Becomes Work*. The average family workload since 1973 increased from 40.6 to 48.8 hours, and like good overachievers, Chuck and I were both above average. Fortunately, our schedules were at least flexible so that one of us was usually home when the boys came home from school; nevertheless, I was often tired and stressed, especially with the continual pile of papers to grade in the evenings and on weekends.

All right, God. Just for kicks. You know my teaching work

overwhelms me at times. Give me the strength to handle it, or help me find something else. You know how much I love to read and write—help me find more time for that. Help me grow as a writer and find an audience with my writing.

Help us know what to do about the puppy and the Nova.

And yes, God, help me relax. Help me to trust.

My thoughts began to swirl like a puppy before a nap. My eyes traced the blues and greens and reds of the Christmas tree lights. I drifted asleep.

Later that week, after we picked up the restored Nova and the puppy from the animal shelter, Chuck and I considered borrowing someone's video camera to capture the boys as they caught their first glimpse of their Christmas presents. But neither of us wanted to be distanced from the moment by a camera. Still, Jesse's shocked brown eyes at the sight of the silver Nova in the driveway, his baritone "For me?" and his uninhibited dance around the car; and then Keegan's eyebrows raised in complete surprise when we opened the car and he saw the kennel, his huge grin, his tender stroking of the bewildered puppy, his naming her "Ginger Lucy" after we told him about the young woman's tears—the photographs in our minds will never yellow, will never be chewed up, will never be lost.

CHAPTER 9

Sax and Sartre

1998

On a late Sunday afternoon in winter, I rushed to prepare the next day's discussion of Sartre and existentialism for my Literature and the Search for Identity class. What I really wanted to do was practice my sax before the night's rehearsal. After a quarter-century hiatus as a musician, I was finally living my fantasy: playing alto sax in a jazz band. It filled me up, just like spending time in nature.

First, though, I had to prepare for the next day's class. I pondered how to illustrate Sartre's concepts of "being-for-myself" and "being-for-the-other." Sartre said there are moments during which we become aware of the "Look": Someone is scrutinizing and possibly evaluating us. We realize then that we are "Object" to their "Subject," and we become vulnerable and self-conscious. We can react to the "Look" in two possible ways: with shame or with pride. When I react with shame, I engage in "being-for-the-other." When I react with pride, I am "being-for-myself."

As I thought about explaining these concepts to my students, I remembered a Fourth of July parade ten years earlier when I was still in my relative youth—barely into my thirties, middle- and old-age distant dots on the horizon. Chuck, Jesse, Keegan, and I stood along a crowded street in Coralville, watching a long parade: cars with banners advertising businesses and politicians, school bands, the ever-present Shriners on tiny motorcycles. Then the float I can still visualize filled with senior citizens in straw hats trimmed with red, blue, and white ribbons. They played "You're a Grand Old Flag" on banjos, a drum, and guitars. A thin-boned woman banging on the tambourine caught my attention.

Her eyes sparkled with abandon as she hit the tambourine in perfect rhythm. "I want to be her someday" was my immediate thought. If I must grow old, I want to be her—enjoying the moment and not caring what others think of my silliness.

That woman was being for herself. I decided to use her as an example in class.

My students, mostly eighteen or nineteen, would like Sartre and his atheism, his insistence that religion and society hold no answers. Our freedom to make meaning for ourselves causes anxiety and despair but ultimately gives us dignity. Knowing the anxiety of young adulthood, some of my students would become Sartre's disciples, at least for a while. But the corner that Sartre painted us into was that of permanent despair. While he emphasized the grand possibility of each individual, it was easy to be depressed by his insistence that we each make our own meaning. Some of my students wrote about making bad choices because of the loneliness and anxiety they carried. One student alluded to drug use in his writing; not long after, he tragically crashed his car into a telephone pole and died.

For me, it was the religious existentialist who resonated. Paul Tillich, the twentieth-century Protestant philosopher, said that we not only experience anxiety and despair but also agony because we intuit that there is a transcendent reality available, a new level of being and existence. Tillich said we cannot experience that transcendence on our own. Divinity is involved. Only a faith in a divine can get us there, not just the faculty of reason, which was so important to Sartre.

I finished preparing for class, warmed up on my sax, and left for rehearsal. About a dozen of us showed that night, many of us parents of youths in the junior and senior high band programs. The summer before, we had drafted the beloved junior high director, Jerry, into leading the band.

Jerry asked Lyle to kick off the first tune with a drum intro. Lyle ran the local office of a large newspaper. He sat behind and to my right, his cymbals clanging, his long, gray-black hair swinging to the beat. Steve worked at the College of Law and stared intently at his guitar music while we played. Les, an engineer and a tall man, even sitting down, added his deep bari sax tones.

As the formerly nimble-fingered high school clarinetist, I

was frustrated to find myself blowing wrong notes as a second-part alto sax player. But I was coming to appreciate the lower register and harmony I could contribute. Besides, Stacy, an ESL teacher and the first-chair sax, was good—always right there on note, rhythm, and tone whether it was Ellington, Nestico, or Count Basie.

Tonight we were preparing for our first gig. We broke into another tune. Mike and Scott, back in the trumpet section, carried the melody for a while, then passed it to the saxes, Stacy leading. Now the trombones layered in.

Somewhere in the middle of this tune, chills crawled up my spine, and I experienced the bliss that keeps musicians playing. I smiled inwardly. I knew that the "look" would come with our first gig, potentially turning us into "objects"—rusty, silly-looking, middle-aged musicians. We'd all look pretty foolish. Still, these moments of bliss—when I transcended myself and time and became subject—were magic. I didn't care what anybody thought about my off-notes or my expanding waistline; I was just in the groove.

While experiencing this chill, my thoughts returned, once again, to the tambourine lady, whose image helped fuel my energy to organize the band. When I was playing on my saxophone, I was experiencing her flow—the being-for-myself state that Sartre described. I was subject, not object. Clearly, my companions were being-for-themselves too. As Steve riffed on the guitar and the trumpet players effortlessly hit the high notes, as Jerry improvised with throaty tones on the tenor sax, and as Lyle's high-hat clumped, our "subjectness" merged.

And this was where Tillich's transcendent reality came in. Through musical communion with others, I stepped into the realm of divinity. I wanted to share the feel of this moment with those students of mine who clustered outside the doors of campus buildings, smoking cigarettes and wearing haunted expressions. I wanted to give them what I knew. But what I knew wasn't necessarily what they needed to know, and I couldn't teach them in a class what it was that had taken me forty-three years to learn.

Still, at this moment, I knew everything. I was everything. I was beyond me. I was living. I was out of the realm of anxiety and despair and in the realm of God.

CHAPTER 10

Quiet Desperation

1998–99

BY THE TIME JESS WRAPPED UP HIS SENIOR YEAR, WE'D LIVED two years in a new house in Coralville on a hilltop with a panoramic view of oak trees and sky—but with little time to enjoy it.

Chuck had been frantic, meeting with bankers and city officials. The congregation was planning to build a permanent home after renting various buildings for almost a decade. To help fund the new building, the congregation created a before- and after-school childcare program. The business plan looked good on paper, but now my husband was a school principal and back-up cook, bus driver, and janitor as well as preacher, counselor, hospital chaplain, and church administrator. Suddenly, his hair was salted with gray.

Everything was rushed. At work I felt cheated out of our dwindling family time as Jess prepared for college. At home I felt the weight of work undone. So much good in our lives. So little time to savor it.

In my American literature classes, I assigned Thoreau's essay "Life without Principle," in which he wrote, "If I should sell both my forenoons and afternoons to society as most appear to do, I am sure that for me there would be nothing left living for . . . There is no more fatal blunderer than he who consumes the greater part of his life getting a living."

Thoreau proposed a simple life: Work less and spend more time pursuing interests in nature, reading, and writing. My students and I passionately agreed with Thoreau. Yet I was leading the life of quiet desperation he so famously described.

I wanted to teach half-time with prorated pay and benefits. However, my being allowed to do so would blur the distinction between the haves—well-paid faculty—and the have-nots—adjunct faculty who worked without benefits, job security, and at a considerably lower pay rate per class.

So I minded my teaching, advising, and committee responsibilities; attended Jess and Keegan's school activities; helped organize soccer tournaments and prom after-parties; and took up the slack at home around Chuck's frenzied schedule.

That May we took time out to celebrate Jesse's high school graduation. Chuck made an elaborate brunch of omelets, tortilla wraps, fresh fruit, and pastries. People filled our spacious house, spilling out onto the deck and the patio below. Jesse's high school friends streamed in, graduation party-hopping their way through Coralville and Iowa City.

"Come see the shrine," I joked, filing everyone past photos I'd mounted on poster boards: a smiling newborn Jess; at four, leaning against a tree, debonair and serious in a white tux and gray cummerbund, ready to hand the rings to the bride and groom at an outdoor wedding; at six, in a jean jacket and a new backpack, hugging Keegan before boarding the school bus, the first day of kindergarten; at seven, Jess clowning in red heart-shaped sunglasses, Keegan watching him mug for the camera.

Family and friends from Iowa Falls made the three-hour trek, including all four of our parents who had so tenderly cared for Jess and Keegan as babies and preschoolers. Iowa City friends offered hugs to our new graduate and to Chuck and me. There was no time to brood that day, only to gaze proudly at our handsome, brown-eyed son as he graciously received well-wishers.

The fall after Jess left for college at Drake University in Des Moines, I teared up during an annual physical with my physician as I told her how worn out I was. Immediately, she suggested Prozac. "I don't need Prozac!" I said. "I just need my life!" I told her about my efforts to negotiate with the college for a half-time job at half my salary. "Why should I go on medication just to keep being a machine?" I asked.

She patted my hand. "I hope it works out."

Reading Thoreau and about the growing Voluntary Simplicity Movement fueled different thinking about life as a teacher, mother, and pastor's wife: My problem was a symptom of a sick lifestyle encouraged—indeed, almost imposed—by society.

Paul Wachtel, in *The Poverty of Affluence*, argued that our preoccupation with economic growth involves a neurotic "miscalculation as to what really works to provide us with security and satisfaction."

I had thought my job would both pay for my family's material needs and provide me with the highest fulfillment. It did—but it was also overwhelming. I had taken a job bigger than I—with busy husband and active sons—could handle without exhaustion.

If Wachtel helped me see my own burnout in a broader light, writer Duane Elgin helped me understand what others were doing about this societal problem. Religious communities such as Quakers have long advocated simple living, but it was Elgin who popularized the term "voluntary simplicity." In his 1981 book of the same name, he argued that a voluntary simplification of lifestyle is the only way to revitalize our ecology—and ourselves. Voluntary simplicity, wrote Elgin, is "a manner of living that is outwardly more simple and inwardly a more rich way of being in which our most authentic and alive self is brought into direct and conscious contact with living."

Those who choose simpler living tend to spend more time with friends, family, and in community service, wrote Elgin. They enjoy the physical, emotional, intellectual, and spiritual realms. They feel more connected to the Earth and to the poor. They consume fewer material things and look for products that are functional, repairable, recyclable, and nonpolluting. They eat healthier, simpler foods and choose environmentally friendly transportation.

These qualities were all attractive to me; I was just too busy to pursue them.

Without the option to reduce my work schedule, I asked myself what else I was called to do. I had not forgotten that inner nudge I had experienced when Chuck had announced his desire to be a minister fourteen years earlier: "Support Chuck. Trust that it will work. You, too, will find your calling."

"Each person enters the world called," wrote psychologist James Hillman in *The Soul's Code: In Search of Calling and Character*. "A sense of personal calling, that there is a reason [we are] alive is lost in too many lives and must be recovered." Hearing him read from his book at Prairie Lights, Iowa City's independent bookstore, I was captivated. Traditional psychology has failed society in its emphasis on dysfunction and childhood trauma, Hillman said. He urged us instead to review our early years for signs of a calling. We may be called to do certain things, he said, or to be of a certain character. Often, he said, our calling shows up in puzzle pieces that emerge in youth and can be pieced together.

Motherhood had been a calling for me, but now our nest was half-empty, and Keegan would graduate in just three years. Yet I couldn't just hang on teaching full-time during those three years. I wanted my life back now. I wanted to savor Keegan's high school years, not just survive them.

I went back over my childhood and youth, looking for clues of a calling other than teaching. It wasn't difficult. I'd always been attracted to the tools of writing: paper, pens, desks, keyboards. In fourth grade I taught myself how to type on my father's old manual typewriter. I spent hours writing stories, working up to sixty words per minute by the end of fifth grade. In junior high I scribbled poetry by the notebook-full. In college I took writing classes, but knowing most writers needed day jobs, I pursued teaching. As it turned out, teaching left little time for writing. I missed writing and the reflection that went with it.

Chuck thrived on fast-paced work mingled with family activities. He could enjoy watching one of the boys' soccer games, then quickly transition back to work. But to be me, I needed time each day to write, reflect, draw, create, contemplate, and appreciate the natural world and my lovely world of family, friends, and colleagues.

I knew this intuitively at age eighteen when I sat day after day in the wooded bird sanctuary in my hometown. Now, as an adult, the obstacles seemed insurmountable. We needed at least half my income for living expenses and our part of Jesse's college costs. Professional part-time jobs with decent pay and benefits were rare, even in progressive Iowa City.

But my readings and reflections about voluntary simplicity and a sense of my own calling left me resolved to make a change, to jump out of the plane before I lost my nerve.

Once I decided to jump, the universe seemed to offer a parachute. A few of my essays were published, giving me the confidence to call myself a writer. The fall after Jess graduated from high school and after nine years of teaching, I found a half-time academic advising position, with benefits, at the University of Iowa.

On my days off, I took Ginger to the woods, where she romped and I strolled and enjoyed the ever-changing colors.

Then I spent the rest of the day writing: essays, a poem, a novel, a collaborative project with another writer. My aim was just to write, not to earn a living by it; even so, several freelance writing opportunities immediately materialized.

I did more housework and ran more errands, leaving more time for Chuck and me to enjoy family and friends. He played soccer in an adult league, and I continued to play sax in the jazz band. We attended a monthly book group together. We relaxed more.

The adjustment wasn't always easy. My influence on students declined when I left the classroom. I lost power and status. I felt less important and more financially vulnerable.

But my most "authentic and alive self" was "brought into direct and conscious contact with living," just as Elgin had written.

It would have been nice to have felt both important and alive. But if I had to make a choice between the two—and right then that seemed to be the case—I chose feeling alive.

No Prozac necessary.

CHAPTER 11

Ministers' Wives

2001

"I WANT TO WANT TO BE THERE," I SAID, WRINKLING MY NOSE at Chuck on a Sunday in March. He'd swooped home after church to grab a bite of bland food and now was throwing on his coat to go back and rearrange the sanctuary for the afternoon gathering. The Iowa bishop and all district clergy, their spouses, and lay leaders were invited to the annual gathering, to be held this year at Chuck's church to celebrate the new building.

"Two hours, though," I said. "Ouch. What is the bishop going to say for two hours?"

Chuck put on his Baptist preacher voice. "'Sue Kelsey,' he'll say, 'You make a damned good bowl of soup. Thank you, Jesus!'"

The flu had struck us both in the middle of the night on Friday. Saturday we woozed motionless all day, Chuck in the recliner, me on the sofa. I'd skipped church that morning but now, as I picked at my potato soup, I felt much better. There was probably no excuse for the minister's wife not to show up for the bishop.

I winced and repeated, "I mean, I really do want to want to be there."

Chuck stroked my matted hair. "You don't have to. Just get better. Stay home and rest."

After he left I slowly rinsed our lunch dishes. The flu had progressed to Keegan, our high school senior. Now, as he took his 7UP into the family room to watch a movie, he joked, "I'm glad I have a real excuse not to go to church this afternoon."

"Lucky boy," I muttered.

I surveyed the messy living room: newspapers all over, empty glasses, and half-full mugs of tea. But the light was streaming in the windows, and I gazed at the ravine of oak trees to the south, the copper tips of their branches hinting at spring. I sat on the sofa, bathing in the sun.

The church-building process helped Chuck grow networking skills with developers, city planners, architects, builders, and city councils, and these skills had benefited our family. The developer had offered us an excellent price for our new house two blocks north of the church, allowing us to move out of our crowded duplex two years before Jess left home. Many Methodist churches provide housing for their clergy, but Chuck's congregation was too young and too new to afford a mortgage on a parsonage. That meant we were benefitting from the equity buildup, not the church. I had worried that people would see our house as an extension of the church, but my worries were unfounded: The congregation was respectful of our privacy.

Feeling grateful, and stomach now settled, I stepped into the shower. I would go this afternoon and support my husband while he had the pleasure of showing off the new building.

And so I stood at the doorway to the sanctuary, the accidental minister's wife, standing by Chuck, shaking hands with people streaming in. The bishop arrived, and I reintroduced myself.

"We met several years earlier at a dinner party in Cedar Rapids," I said.

"Yes, I remember your face," he said, kindly. "I'm not as good at names." A handsome man in his late fifties, he had an engaging smile. I knew the ministers in the crowd would draw energy from the bishop's presence. He would affirm their work, which could be grueling and challenging and was always ongoing.

A clergywoman who had driven from an hour away walked in the door and steadied herself against the wall. I recognized this as the flu in its early stages. I shook her hand and welcomed the other 200 clergy and spouses with cheerful enthusiasm. Internally, I willed them all to have a good two hours—two hours!—here and to be renewed in their work.

The chatting crowd milled into the sanctuary. Chuck had hired a jazz trio: a string bassist, a pianist, and a drummer. They played jazz standards such as "Take the 'A' Train" and "Mood Indigo." As they began "Days of Wine and Roses," I winked at Chuck, now across the room shaking hands with peers. The trio turned to a few gospel-jazz charts, playing versions of "Come Sunday" and "Amazing Grace," the crowd clapping approval after every song. I looked at my watch and realized nearly an hour had gone by. Relatively painless so far.

Eventually, the distinguished bishop stepped to the pulpit and gave his sermon, a rousing half-hour pep talk to the team. The flu woman zealously nodded her head, just like the springy dashboard Jesus—a gift from a parishioner—that Chuck kept in his office.

We sang three hymns after the sermon, rich harmony from a sea of serious O-shaped mouths. From the row behind me, I heard a beautiful tenor voice and turned around to steal a glance at a large man about fifty with gray hair. After the service, he sat alone at the back of the room, so I walked up and said hello and introduced myself. More uncharacteristic behavior from the introverted pastor's wife.

The man poured forth with information as if I had touched a button that said, "Press and I'll tell you my life story." He was new to the ministry, he said, but he and his wife were separated because she didn't like being a minister's wife.

"Oh, really?" I said.

"She thinks I give my best to everyone else and she gets the leftovers," he said, disbelief in his voice. "She sees the congregation as competition!" His large blue eyes were incredulous—but maybe also a little pleased?

I nodded, thinking back to that Sunday morning early in Chuck's ministry when the beautiful woman touched the pewter peace pin on his suit lapel and the way Chuck's step backward just might have saved our marriage. I felt protective of this man's absent wife.

"We are best friends," he said. "I don't want to spend the rest of my life with anyone else."

I looked around. Why was he confiding in me?

"When she told me she couldn't be a minister's wife anymore, she knew what my answer would be. I have been called, and I'm not going to turn my back on my calling." I imagined a large hand scooping him up from the sky while he waved goodbye to his wife as she grew smaller and smaller.

"These issues are very familiar" was my lame offering. "Maybe a counselor could help you communicate."

I didn't know him well enough to say more, such as that his wife needed to know that he would make time for her, and for himself, too, or he would be no good to anyone. Or that he should train the congregation to respect his family time. Or that his numbers might not grow as large and fast in his church if he prioritized his marriage. But were numbers really God's bottom line anyway?

"I do wish you and your wife all the best as you sort this out," I said. And then I scanned the emptying sanctuary, looking for Chuck. I knew he had to run to the hospital; a parishioner's father had suffered a massive stroke. The next few weeks would be hectic; an out-of-town funeral would take two days while all his other work fell behind. And Easter was coming up.

But I knew that Chuck would find time for me in the week ahead. And if he didn't, I had my ways. "Please, Reverend," I might say, "can't you skip that meeting about how many angels can dance on the head of a pin?" I couldn't always count on Chuck to remember to stop home and let the dog out, but I could count on him to find time for his family. I knew he would make time for all of Keegan's soccer games that spring. I knew we would find time to walk along the Coralville Reservoir.

It had been a rocky twelve years since Chuck had entered the ministry, but we had weathered the new church start and the new building because we made time for each other. Luckily, so far the Methodist itinerancy had not come into play, so we had been able to stay in our beloved Iowa City to finish raising our sons. Keegan would graduate in two months.

I shook the good tenor's hand, then moved toward Chuck. I was proud of him. His peers had celebrated the new building for which he had worked so hard. I gazed at the empty sanctuary, pleased by the simple lines: the unadorned, rectangular shape; the peaked roof; the simple, large windows with a beautiful panoramic view of rolling Iowa hills, now pale green. As I returned home to make Keegan some chicken noodle soup, I whispered a prayer for the man with the beautiful tenor voice. And then a longer prayer for his dear best friend—the lucky minister's wife.

CHAPTER 12

Praying with the Fundamentalists

2001

I WAVED THE CHURCH NEWSLETTER AT CHUCK WHEN HE entered the house, cleared my throat, and read, "'Pray for Pastor Chuck and his wife, Sue, for guidance against the Evil One.' Is there something I don't know?"

His dimples appeared. "That's the new prayer team, Laura and Carol. I asked them to write a column. They're on the conservative side. Carol was Southern Baptist, I think. Not sure about Laura."

Outside our living room window, green oak leaves fanned a hazy, humid Iowa sky in mid-August.

"Maybe they think my empty nest blues are a battle with Satan," I mused. Keegan had just left for his first year of college in Illinois, and I had admitted to Carol I was having a hard time.

"Or they think we're too liberal. Or I'm too casual about skipping church." I smile-frowned at Chuck. "It's like they think we're about to commit a crime or have an affair."

"I know, but I want them to do it their way," Chuck said. He smiled again.

"But 'The Evil One'? Sounds like Darth Vader." I tossed the newsletter in the recycling pile as I walked past him, ignoring his handsome dimples.

After church the next Sunday, I stood with Laura by the coffeepot at the back of the sanctuary. In her mid-forties like me, she looked like an ash-blonde Bette Midler. "Laura," I said, "I'm curious about the prayer in the newsletter, the one that asked for guidance for Chuck and me against 'The Evil One.' Are we in some kind of struggle I don't know about?"

"No!" she said as her sky-blue eyes widened in surprise. "That's just a prayer of protection since Chuck is the church leader and you're his wife." Her voice was the timbre of a viola. "Leaders are especially vulnerable to attacks."

"Attacks?"

"Yes. Satan doesn't want God's church to grow, so leaders are often tested." She looked as if she were stating the obvious.

"Oh." I took a breath. The sanctuary smelled of strong coffee and extinguished candles. "I've never heard conflict or evil personified like that in the Methodist Church."

"Really?" Laura's fair-skinned face turned red. "I apologize. Methodists do think differently, don't they? I was raised in an Assembly of God congregation. My family and I feel we're called to this church for some reason. But I want to be able to speak everybody's language with the prayers we put in the newsletter. Maybe I should ask Pastor Chuck to edit them."

"Please, don't apologize." I said, touching her arm. "I was just curious."

For years, besides my agnosticism, my teaching job had been my excuse for erratic church attendance. But now that I had more time, with our empty nest and my flexible work schedule, shouldn't I be showing up more, especially since Chuck was trying so valiantly and against all odds to make this church grow? I wasn't sure, and so I was faking it until I was. Somehow, it felt like Laura knew things that I did not.

Augustine wrote that language both separates us from God and is the point of contact with God. He thought people tended to be drawn to either the kataphatic way of revelation through images, language, and thoughts or to the apophatic way that transcends language and image and, instead, enters into God's mystery through love.

As a writing and literature teacher, and now a writer with a growing freelancing business, I made my living with words but had never been comfortable with Christian rhetoric. I thought it was becoming even more canned, cliché, and patriarchal via

Jerry Falwell and other members of the Religious Right who held conservative positions on school prayer, homosexuality, and abortion. I was drawn to the apophatic way—the nameless, the indescribable, the mystical. For me, this intuitive sense of the divine was most apparent in nature.

But I was curious about Carol and Laura. They seemed so sure, so confident in their churchgoing faith. They leaned right and I leaned left; still, maybe I could learn something from them.

They advertised their Intercessory Prayer Group in the church newsletter: a group of people who would gather weekly to pray for their needs and the needs of the congregation. I decided to join.

We were an unlikely bunch. Laura punctuated our prayers with "Yes, Jesus!" Carol had a tinkling laugh but made firm appeals to God. Hannah was a quiet physician raised in a charismatic church where members spoke in tongues and waved hands as signs of God's presence, and yet enigmatically she was also an ardent feminist who performed occasional abortions. And then there was me, the elusive minister's wife.

We met on Wednesday evenings in a small room off the church sanctuary. Laura and Carol turned off the ceiling light, lit candles, and draped a scarf over a floor lamp, creating a quiet spot. Carol, her face shadowed by the lighting, opened with a Bible reading, then asked us to check in with celebrations and concerns from the week.

"I helped deliver three babies and all went well," Hannah reported.

"Praise God!" Laura whispered.

"But I'm concerned about threats the family planning clinic has been getting lately. I ask for prayers of protection for the people who work there."

If Carol and Laura had qualms with Hannah's work at the clinic, they said nothing. The unspoken agreement to disagree helped me feel comfortable, despite our theological differences. Carol simply nodded and wrote down Hannah's concern. "Laura?"

"My neighbor is battling cancer. And my daughter Sally sounds unhappy at college. I'm not sure it's the best place for her, so I ask God to help her sort that out."

"Sue?"

"World peace?"

Carol laughed. "We have to get you up to speed, girl! You've got to be more specific! Remember, it says in Matthew 7:8: 'For everyone who asks receives, the one who seeks finds, and to the one who knocks, the door will be opened.'"

I took a breath and reluctantly shared a couple of concerns. Keegan would be balancing Division I soccer at Bradley University with a demanding load of classes. I worried he wouldn't eat nutritious foods or get enough sleep. Jess, who had transferred to the University of Iowa, was working a lot of hours and trying to decide what to do after his senior year.

"There you go, that's more like it!" Carol said, making notes. "Now does anyone have any prayers for the congregation?"

Hannah wanted prayers for the church youth group program.

Laura asked for prayers for Pastor Chuck to make good decisions as the church leader. I cringed as always at the appellation of "Pastor Chuck." Why couldn't people just call him Chuck? But at least she hadn't mentioned the "Evil One."

There were requests for prayers for other groups in the church, for the Iowa City and Coralville community, and for university students who might be homesick or struggling in school.

Then we joined hands around the table and bowed our heads. Carol spoke: "We pray for Sally, that you will give her direction for her future. Help her to know where her place is."

Hannah began to whisper something I couldn't make out.

When one went silent, another picked up the strand of concerns. "Help this church grow, God." "Help the right people move into positions of leadership." "Help attract people who will benefit from the church and who will help us reach out to the community."

More silence, then Carol rolled into a twenty-minute finale. "Father God, dear Jesus, we beseech thee." I squirmed in my chair at the King James lilt and references to God as male—something Chuck tried to avoid. "We gather here together as an expression of our faith in thee."

"Yes, Jesus!" whispered Laura.

"And we thank thee for all the blessings you've given us today and during the week."

Hannah continued whispering, perhaps speaking in tongues unobtrusively so I wouldn't freak out. She sounded like she was blowing on kindling to start a fire; suddenly, it made sense to me that the Holy Spirit is often represented by a flame.

"Jesus told us to pray for our needs, God, and that's! what!

we're! doing!" Carol pounded her hands onto the table for emphasis, my knuckles getting rapped in the process since we were holding hands. She repeated some of the requests in a soft pianissimo, added her own, wove in several Bible verses, her voice now in a slow crescendo, and now reminding God, in a slightly threatening forte, of God's promises to answer prayers. Hannah fanned the fire; Carol had it crackling, and she prayed loudly for at least another twenty minutes. I shifted in my chair again; I had things to do at home. Finally, Carol was silent, and then, "And in Jesus's name we pray, Amen."

"Amen," we said. We sat silently for a minute, then stood and hugged each other. We blew out the candles and turned out the lamp. Worries and concerns had swirled up and away; my steps were light as I left the dark building.

We continued this way each week on Wednesday evenings. While the others prayed to Jesus, I addressed a more feminine God in my mind. But we were united by our desire to be heard. I think Carol and Laura expected God to pony up, but they also accepted "nos" if their requests did not reflect God's will.

In her essay "Singing with the Fundamentalists," writer Annie Dillard describes singing every morning with a group of college students where she taught. "The main thing about them is: 'There isn't any them,'" she wrote. "Their views vary." As I prayed with these women, I came to the same conclusion.

It did feel good to set my box of concerns on the table once a week and pray about them. I recognized the paradox of praying to a God who seems to take away as much as She gives. Even so, unloading the box, however briefly, was better than carrying it all the time.

When our prayers were answered, we celebrated. "This is why I write them down," a jubilant Carol said after Hannah told us that our prayers for help in passing her board re-certifications had been answered. "It increases my faith and helps me remember to thank God. God answers prayers. The ones God doesn't answer, we can just keep asking for. When God doesn't answer our prayers, that's when we have to trust there's a bigger picture that we cannot see."

Eventually, I left the group. I'd stretched myself by entering the territory of "Praise God" and "We beseech thee, Jesus" to know more about that way of being—and to appreciate it. But it wasn't in me to stay. I learned they were sure because that's who they were; I wasn't sure because it wasn't my nature to be.

I went back to my silent communion with the divine while walking in the woods, where I mostly listened. But sometimes I also spoke to God about my concerns. Even when my prayer requests weren't answered or my words seemed to fall on divine-but-deaf ears, I felt at least momentarily better for having emptied the box. When the answer seemed to be no, I tried to remember that there might indeed be a larger picture, as Carol said. When my pleas were answered, I smiled and thought of her beautiful hand writing down the requests so she could remember to be grateful.

And I was.

CHAPTER 13

The Nature of Disturbance

2002

AS I SHIFTED FROM TEACHER TO WRITER AND CONTEMPLATIVE, I still wrestled with my relationship to the church. At forty-four, I envied those who got something out of organized religion other than the feeling of being rubbed the wrong way. I felt like Goldilocks: this doctrine too narrow, that organ music too loud, these people way too serious.

By chance, fate, or divine intervention, a friend invited me to meet monthly with Buddhists, a Catholic, Episcopalians, a Lutheran, atheists, agnostics, a Hindu, and a newly converted Muslim to discuss books on spirituality and mysticism.

Twelve of us sipped tea in a crowded circle in Cindy's living room while her stereo played a cello adagio. We discussed *Dialogues with a Modern Mystic*, in which writer Mark Matousek interviewed Andrew Harvey, an Anglo-Indian poet, scholar, and mystic. Bob, a philosophy professor, agreed with Harvey that the free market economy devastates the environment and that Western culture should turn to the sacred feminine and a mystical reverence for the natural to revive the wounded planet.

Deirdre, an economist and transsexual new to both womanhood and spiritual quest, thought Harvey exaggerated. "Most of the land in this world is still uninhabited," she said, patting her strawberry blonde hair, "and no one agrees about the state of the environment and whether global warming is truly a concern." As I stared at her large hands and painted fingernails, my mind wandered from the sacred feminine to feminine aesthetics. The tight knit dress snugged onto her large frame contrasted with the loose layers worn by most of my female peers.

Bob insisted the Earth was in danger. I, too, was surprised by the conservative argument coming from a person who had undergone such a radical revision of her body. From newspaper articles, I knew that even though her body as a male was perfectly and acceptably masculine, Deirdre had chosen to become a female with painful surgeries and body hair removal. Her life and mine couldn't have been more different, but I recognized in her a companion—both of us foreigners in our own lands, expected to live inauthentically: in her case, as a man; in mine, as a church lady.

The bladed tension in Cindy's living room between Bob and Deirdre softened, and soon the two were smiling at each other. A fortyish man named Michael changed the subject in a hesitating, almost whispered cadence. "Has anyone... experienced any... mystical moments as described by Harvey?"

Ken, a dark-haired engineer in his thirties, spoke up. "I had one brought on by severe pain actually. I was outdoors on top of a hill, pounding nails into a shed I was building. I had a board across my leg, trying to remove a misplaced nail. I wasn't paying close attention, and I hammered my kneecap. The pain was terribly intense—so much that I knew I couldn't allow myself to feel it.

"I looked across the valley to the trees and hills on the other side. And suddenly, I was aware of the beauty and of the fact that I was completely united with this landscape. It was very clear to me that I was part of the whole." His voice cracked and his eyes reddened. "I'm sorry. This happened years ago, but it still breaks me up to think about it. I was in a complete state of awe until the pain began to subside. I've never experienced anything like it again."

I was then too shy to share my own mystical moments, which had been visiting me regularly since resigning my teaching position. I now had time—deep time—to write and to hike daily with our dog, Ginger, along the Coralville Reservoir, on trails at the MacBride Field Campus north of Iowa City, and at Palisades-Kepler Park east of Cedar Rapids. In these places of forest, postage-stamp prairie, and water, I easily found the divine grace that Chuck and I believed in, each in our own way.

The universe seemed to affirm my decision to follow my

calling by revealing its divinity on a regular basis. During early morning walks in the woods, I experienced startling revelations of beauty. The sun's cast of shadows on the emerging yellow-green leaves, the ripples of lake water, the perfume of the sweet Williams—it all engaged me with intense joy. These nature-induced ecstasies were relief from a too-busy life and my guilt about being a renegade minister's wife. The daily walks also began to heal me from what I didn't even know ailed me: the bleak natural landscape of my childhood. In north central Iowa, except for riparian fringes along the Iowa River and the sweet alfalfa pastures here and there, the land is flat and monotonous, trees long ago felled and marshes drained for fencerow-to-fencerow farming, leaving endless corn and soybean fields. In the late Octobers of my youth, the fields went black after fall plowing, earning that part of the state the nickname Black Desert. After leaving the area, I never missed the flat sterility, nor the no-nonsense way of those who made their living on it, nor the way I was taught to romanticize a chemical-dependent agricultural system that has left the state's waters among the most polluted in the nation.

I fell in love with the hills of southeast Iowa and the way the harder-to-farm topography yielded generous, wild growth. Hiking the rolling woods and along rivers and prairies, I felt a divine presence that had eluded me in church. An inner guide that I equated with God, though it could have been just my sharpened intuition (they seemed the same, to me), gently kept me company, helped me see the beauty in the landscape, teased me into parting with any worries for the day, even helped me plan my writing. I could genuinely worship here, not as cowering subservient but as one in awe of creation. Sometimes I sensed that if God had feelings, She might be lonely because so few people see the way prairies are laced with Her little surprises, like the vivid blue bottle gentians hiding in waving grasses.

I liked that Andrew Harvey calls experiences like mine in nature, or like Ken's in pain, "mystical" because they are a direct experience of God. Harvey describes a Sufi saint who went into ecstasy upon seeing just one rose. "His disciples would try to clear all the flowers out of the room; otherwise they wouldn't get any teaching. If his eyes strayed to one of the ragged flowers in the bowls in the corner, he would be out for the rest of the afternoon." I, too, was intoxicated with the time and solitude to truly see divine beauty.

Harvey warns that an addiction to mystical experiences "can end in a subtle grief, in which you are longing for bliss" and miss out on life. A period of frequent mystical revelations, he says, is often only a phase in one's spiritual journey. Listening to Ken that night, I vowed to appreciate my mystical gifts while they lasted.

Next month at Deirdre's, the uninhibited Michael asked, "How many of us are really present in this moment?" He was a former Transcendental Meditation practitioner who abandoned TM when his peers blamed an insufficiency in his practice for causing his cancer. Now in remission, he had survived long past his physician's expectations. His solid, 6'5" body belied any trace of illness. Tossing his long, sun-bleached hair, he said, "This question has recently become my spiritual riddle, my koan. But I'm puzzled. Are we each really individuals or are we all one in different manifestations? I don't know whether I am totally alone or part of a whole." Then he closed his eyes—his habit when listening.

Someone finally offered the Hindu idea that we're not-one, yet we're not-two. Harvey's example is the sea:

> Look at the sea. All waves are rising and falling differently, in different rhythms, with different volumes. Some catch the light, some do not. You can see the separations between the waves, but what you also see quite clearly is that all the waves are water. That is what the knowledge of "not-two" is like.

Deirdre, her eyes sparkling beneath blue eye shadow, said "If we're not-two, that means I don't have to share as many of these." She grabbed a cookie from the silver tray on the coffee table. Michael smiled, his eyes still closed, while the rest of us roared with laughter.

At Laurie's house another month, we discussed Catholic priest Henry Nouwen's *The Genesee Diary: Report from a Trappist Monastery*. Cindy was grateful to learn that the priest's life was not much different from her own as an engineer and a single mother. "His struggles make mine feel more normal." Nouwen's book documents the seven months he spent in a monastery and is filled with reports of the simple joy of washing raisins for the commercial bread-baking operation. But he also discusses his battles with anger, ego, and greed, and this comforted Cindy.

We all liked Nouwen's decision toward the end of the book: Instead of struggling against who he is, he decides to be who he is. He says:

> We live because we share God's breath, God's life, God's glory. The question is not so much, "How to live for the Glory of God?" but, "How to live who we are, how to make true our deepest self?"

Someone asked, "What if the truest, deepest self is evil?" We found questions like this mostly unanswerable. We agreed to assume that Nouwen was writing about relatively whole people with everyday faults and about learning to accept our defects as part of our wholeness.

Eventually, we wandered into Laurie's kitchen for food— part of each month's ritual. Arranged artfully on the table were a brownie cake and an oblong wooden bowl of red strawberries, the shiny dimpled berries a pleasing contrast to the smooth, unlacquered wood. I grabbed some of the offerings and returned to the living room where Ken, Michael, and Cindy chatted with Sara, a new attendee in her late twenties. Sara said, "I've had a tough time adjusting to my seven-to-five work schedule. I realize now it was such a luxury in grad school to stay up until midnight to study and then sleep in mornings. It seems now like there's no time for prayer, for exercise, for people."

Ken agreed. "Nouwen's physical labor at the monastery gave him praying-by-hand time," he said, "but my day is so consumed with mental work that I can't be contemplative. And at the end of the day, I'm mentally exhausted."

We all nodded. How to live who we are, how to make true our deepest selves? I felt a twinge of guilt at finally having more time in my own life to be contemplative. But I was a decade older than Ken and almost twice as old as Sara. I, too, had been too busy—for twenty-five years, my entire adulthood. When Ken and Sara reached my age, they, too, might trade their good-paying careers for their deepest selves.

In the silence, I thought about how I found this group's willingness to question more sacred than listening to anyone's sermon—even Chuck's. (How can you take seriously a man who hikes up his boxers and dives into bed at night?) Through the group's questioning and seeking, I was becoming convinced that whatever the tradition, a core of mystical, ecumenical divinity flowed underneath, over, and around everything—like Harvey's sea, only invisible. In that core resided the fundamental principles of all religions: The triumph of love over fear. The need to trust in something greater than ourselves. The need to practice compassion.

Beneath it all, holding everything together, is that flowing, invisible water of love, mystery, and beauty.

The reading group helped me admit that Chuck's decision to become a minister was one of the worst and best things to ever happen to me. In spite or because of its strangeness and loss of privacy, his choice demanded that I listen harder to myself. Because of his disturbance, I was growing organically and aggressively—first out of self-defense, then out of compassion, and finally out of understanding—toward myself.

High species diversity is often found in ecosystems in which disturbances are not too rare but also not too frequent. Annual plowing and planting have reduced 90 percent of Iowa to mostly two plant species—corn and soybeans—where once there had been hundreds of prairie species. But occasional disturbances, such as fire, tornado, flood, drought, or insect outbreak, tend to yield higher species diversity. (Farmers don't want that diversity because it interferes with the crops, but the land wants it and would be healthier for it.) This principle holds true with human nature as well: For healthy internal diversity, we need to be shaken up once in a while.

I returned the disturbance favors to my mate in my own way. Taking the job too seriously is a hazard of his profession, but he simply couldn't do so when I was around. Occasionally, I reminded him, "Forget buying a Harley. Entering the ministry is the only midlife crisis you get." And of course there were all sorts of plays on his title, like adding a "d" to the end of "Pastor."

Because I was finding my own way to explore spirituality outside a religious institution, Chuck could not assume, as do many clergy, that all the unchurched are lost souls. Fortunately for me, he is not an exclusivist who believes Jesus is the only way. We both agree that Christianity is one of many paths to wholeness, and we both think the world needs species diversity in religion and spirituality as much as it does in nature.

In December the book group decided to watch a video at my house instead of reading a book. Michael insisted we see *On Having No Head*. He said he would be late, but since he had already seen the film, we could watch it before he arrived.

In the film, a British man sits in front of a tie-dyed sheet and suggests that we should not take ourselves literally because we can't see ourselves except in the reflection of a mirror or in the ways others respond to us. We shouldn't be as concerned about who we are as we should be about "making space" for others. Others, then, become part of who we are. I thought about Henry Nouwen's suggestion to live who we are and make true our deepest self. This speaker seemed to say the opposite: We should strive to erase our individual selves and, instead, allow others to define us.

"What is Michael's groove on this film?" someone asked.

"This is the kind of spatial, quasi-physics stuff that intrigues him," said someone else.

Michael finally arrived but immediately disappeared into the bathroom. Soon he entered the living room with a paper bag over his head—Michael's tall, muscular body in jeans and a wool sweater without a head, in the spirit of the video. We laughed. It was so—Michael.

He removed the bag and, in his hesitating rhythm, told us he had finally found the answer to his koan about how many people are present in any given moment. The film helped him realize the self was not the place to start. Then, while pondering the word "moment," he realized that every moment is sacred. And since rituals are often invoked for sacred moments, perhaps every moment is a ritual.

"So if every moment—like this one, now—is a ritual, there are always three entities present, according to a Hindu tradition: Hotri, the chanter of the scriptures; Deity, the witness to whom the offering is made; and Potri, the one who performs the ritual."

Ten of us sat silently on the sofa, the chairs, and the floor. We looked at each other. I tested Michael's idea in my mind, dividing us into three entities: Michael now as Potri, the performer of the ritual with his paper bag; the film's speaker as

Hotri, the chanter of the scriptures or the ideas at hand; the rest of us as Deity, the witnesses, however irreverent. Yes, all of us as Deity—merged with God and maybe supernaturally even with Deirdre, who had moved out of town.

Maybe, I thought, we each have a frequency at which we most relate to the Divine, the mystical, invisible sea. Mine is visual: light, pattern, and color, especially in nature, but even a neon green stoplight against evergreens at dusk can send me into a minor ecstasy. Bob, the philosophy professor, was drawn to the environment and Deirdre to a body that now matched her internal gender. Chuck connected to the Methodist Church, bless his soul, and especially to a code of service to the oppressed. Michael seemed tuned to a frequency beyond the limits of the self. Each of us with different frequencies—agnostics, atheists, Christians, Jews, Muslims, Sufis, Hindus, pagans—all of us part of the invisible sea.

Perhaps Michael's koan was a symbol of his search for how to continue to be a part of the ritual of life after he no longer physically existed. Or maybe his cancer was more on my mind than his. Maybe it was his preparation for the rest of us; after anyone left the group, we could look for the person's metaphysical presence at the ritual. Indeed, I didn't know it right then, but Chuck and I would soon be uprooted from the town we loved, courtesy of the Methodist itinerancy.

Michael's boyish radiance touched my heart. And this group of men and women who laughed and cried, sought and fought, we would keep witnessing, chanting, making the offering, every moment a ritual. As Goldilocks, I had finally found a chair that fit. And sometimes while on my walks on the wild side, I thought I saw a sparkle from the invisible sea.

CHAPTER 14

Leaving Home

2002

AFTER BARB PULLED UP IN OUR DRIVEWAY IN EARLY JULY, she handed me a four-inch statue of a man in a robe and told me that according to tradition, burying a St. Joseph statue in our yard would help sell our house. "If nothing else," she said, "maybe he'll add comic relief to the trauma of leaving." She said she'd had luck with the statue in Indiana before her family's move to Iowa City a few years earlier. Since their arrival we'd had many conversations on the sidelines of soccer games.

"How long have you lived in Coralville?" she asked.

"Fourteen years," I said.

She shook her head and pulled a wisp of blonde hair behind her ear. "How long has your house been on the market?"

"Since March, when we found out about the transfer."

"And when is your moving date?"

"Chuck left the first of July. He's already started at the church in Ames. The movers are coming July 31."

"Well, then, you definitely need this. Bury it six inches down." Barb smiled and handed me the little hard-plastic figure she'd kept in a Ziplock bag, Indiana dirt still filling the crevices in the ivory-colored robe. She gave me a trowel, its sturdy metal marked with inches, and then she hopped in her van. I waved and watched her drive away, appreciating her generosity, already missing her melodious laugh.

Shortly after July 4 in a flowerbed behind our house, a few inches north of a fragrant petunia and east of a clump of ornamental grass, I dug a hole for the little St. Joseph statue.

Through three inches of springy peat moss and another three of hard clay, I carefully positioned him upside down, facing the house, as Barb prescribed. Then I straightened up and, more emphatically than necessary, stomped on the dirt above his tiny feet.

I gazed at the back of our house. We'd finished raising Jess and Keegan here, fed their friends and soccer teams, celebrated high school graduations. Jess, almost twenty-three, lived in Iowa City, but he would move to San Francisco in a month. Keegan, nineteen and home for the summer, would soon leave for his sophomore year at college.

Running my fingers through the dirt above St. Joseph, I tried not to think too much about sons leaving. Ginger watched, her plumed tail wagging slightly when I looked at her. "This is not for you to dig," I said sharply. Her ears flattened.

Joseph is the patron saint of real estate. Since he was the father of a Holy House, it makes sense for him to preside over the selling and buying of homes. The Bible says an angel told Joseph that Mary, his fiancée, was pregnant with God's child, though scholars suggest that the idea of a virgin birth was probably borrowed from Greek mythology. Virgin or not, Joseph's job was to stand by Mary and help her raise Jesus. A simple carpenter, Joseph would receive neither accolades nor favors for raising this special child. He would go down in history as a minor player.

I, too, was a minor player, soon to be a trailing spouse. But no angel had warned me that this would be the year the bishop would turn our lives upside down and send Chuck to a large Methodist Church in Ames in central Iowa, the flattest part of the state.

I walked to the patio and sat on the wooden swing hanging under the deck. The swing had been our first purchase six years earlier for the new house, and we had sat in various combinations on these strong wooden slats: Chuck and I after yard work; Keegan and Jess while Chuck grilled dinner on the patio. Sometimes on late, sunny afternoons, after a long day of grading or writing, I threw a quilt and pillow on the swing and reclined to read.

Today, falling into the swing, I sighed, Ginger at my feet.

Maybe Joseph felt a little unimportant making cupboards or tables, as I did writing marketing and technical documents that had become my freelancing bread and butter. But maybe he also craved the comfort of being alone in his workshop, as I did my office. Did we have in common the fact that we needed solitude and that our loved ones were often drawn away from us, off ministering to the crowds?

When Chuck entered the ministry, I knew that the Methodist itinerancy system would eventually dictate this move, but somehow, I had convinced myself we'd be here forever in this house on a hill.

Iowa City had made room for me as a teacher, a colleague, a friend, a volunteer, and a fledgling writer. Iowa City was home, was where I had become me. I pushed off the ground, making the swing fly. Where was my guiding angel, Joseph?

In mid-July I drove the two hours to Ames for Chuck's installation. He and his co-pastor, also new to town, had been conducting worship services for several weeks, but today was the official royal treatment. The church was large and formal, the sanctuary lined with dark pews, the walls covered with stained-glass windows. I felt claustrophobic. I already missed the little church back in Coralville—that brick structure with a peaked roof, the unassuming piano, the windows framing open views of hills and trees.

At the reception people streamed by, shaking our hands, expressing welcomes, and asking me to join things—the Methodist Women's group, the puppet ministry for children's church, the adult Sunday school class. As the invitations accumulated, I became overwhelmed. How did I tell these well-meaning people that I wouldn't be an active minister's wife, that Ginger and I would probably be taking hikes in the woods on Sunday mornings?

A nicely coiffed woman in her mid-sixties grabbed my hand. "Can you and Chuck have supper with us tonight?"

I smiled but shook my head. "Thanks, but I need to head back to Iowa City this afternoon."

"How about lunch then?"

I just wanted to spend a quiet two hours with my husband in our strange new house. I wanted to have some time for us to let some things sink in, and not just about the move. Chuck's beloved Grandma Cord had died in early May at the age of ninety-two. In June, his father had had a heart attack and subsequent bypass surgery. Just weeks earlier my father had been put on oxygen for emphysema. Our own lives had been so hectic, I wasn't sure we'd really registered any of these changes. I just wanted to be quiet together for a couple of hours. And then I wanted to flee back to Iowa City—to home.

Stumbling over my words, I said no as politely as I could.

Chuck and I spent the afternoon in the house—the parsonage. It endeared me that a committee of trustees from the church had spent hours painting the walls off-white, fixing the weather stripping on the doors, and laying light taupe carpet that would hide Ginger's ever-shedding tan hair. On the other hand, the echo of their presence also put me off: all those people in the spaces that Chuck and I would share intimately, their work subtly reminding us that this was their home, not ours.

Yet I liked the two-story house built in the 1940s. The large rectangular windows and their simple white blinds admitted outdoor light filtered by large oaks and maple trees. I liked that the house was nestled in an older neighborhood within walking distance of a quaint Main Street.

"You need to choose your office," Chuck said as we walked hand-in-hand upstairs. We looked in at a huge room over the garage with knotty-pine paneling and plentiful shelves. "This one was built to be the pastor's study, but I'll just use my office at the church like I've always done."

The irony hit me: We'd have more space in this house than ever, but we no longer needed it because our nest was empty.

"This one might be more your style," he said as we moved into the southeast bedroom with two large windows. I liked the light and space. We opened a door and stepped out onto the deck above the downstairs porch; the oak towering over the deck made it feel like a tree house.

"Are you sure you don't want an office at home? It looks like we could each have one, plus still have a guest room."

"Nope, just the kitchen," he said with a smile. He'd always preferred his office at the church to be more accessible to parishioners and people seeking food. This church didn't yet have a food pantry, but I knew he would probably initiate one. It was one of his signature ministries at the church in Coralville. I nodded, taking in his dimples and the light in his warm brown eyes.

While we hugged in my future office, I thought about two things: First, in our twenty-six years of marriage, we'd never lived in a house shaded by a mature tree; and second, I'd missed the comforting feel of my husband's sturdy body. For an hour, I forgot that I'd been angry with him for months for agreeing to itinerate to Ames. Since March I'd toyed with the idea of living in Iowa City while Chuck rode out the next five to seven years in Ames, but I realized it now: I needed to be here. With him.

Just before I left, we reviewed the details of the move. Since our Coralville house wasn't selling, we'd better try to rent it. As I drove back, I debated about whether to put a for rent sign in the yard next to the for sale sign, post an ad on the university website, place an ad in the paper, or all three. Yet another layer of tasks to add to keeping up the house and lawn while trying to meet a fall deadline on a book I was cowriting. Chuck was the reason we were leaving this place I loved so much. Why should I have to handle all his details? I felt the anger creeping back.

JULY 23   Moving day was the next week, but St. Joseph was apparently sleeping on the job. The realtors had steadily shown the house since March. For each showing, I'd stopped my work on the book and loaded Ginger in the van for a walk at the Coralville Reservoir. But we'd had no offers, nor had a single person responded to the rental ad I'd placed in the paper. With a mortgage payment, utilities, and lawn care, the cost of an empty house would add up quickly beginning next week. In Ames we would have free use of the parsonage, but Chuck's salary was also considerably less because of the free housing. I had no idea how soon I'd develop a freelancing base in Ames, but anything I made would go toward Keegan's college expenses and other bills.

I focused on making butter-fudge frosting for brownies after the evening meal. Keegan drove up, yelling "hello" as he ran downstairs to shower after a strenuous soccer workout. His summer schedule was frenetic with electrical work all day for a contractor and soccer practices or weightlifting to keep in shape for his university soccer team. The rest of the evening he spent with his girlfriend or other friends—two lives stuffed into one summer's living. Tonight, though, he had agreed to slow down long enough to have dinner with his brother and me.

Jess drove up. I watched our dark-haired son walk up the driveway with a little smile. Stepping into the house, his arms flew up, Olympic-athlete style, as he announced in his baritone, "Two more classes and I'm done."

"Almost a college grad!" I said, giving him a hug. "And turning twenty-three in three weeks."

"And heading west very shortly," he said, grinning widely now.

As if I needed a reminder, I thought. "You have much to smile about," I said, taking a breath, resolving not to let my sadness about his leaving infect our dinner. "Want to cut these?"

"Sure." He stepped up to the wooden table in the center of the kitchen and began chopping vegetables in the expert way of his father. "How was your day?" he asked.

I talked about the book, about the frustrations of getting interrupted but the joys of working with my cowriter, an eighty-three-year-old man who had coached fifty years at Grinnell College. I had been hired by the college to help Coach Pfitsch tell funny, endearing, poignant stories about his athletes.

Keegan bounded up the stairs and entered the kitchen. His light brown hair was uncombed, his t-shirt damp. "Hey, bro," he said, patting Jesse on the back. "What's for supper, Mama?" His term of endearment for me. My blue-eyed son was evidently feeling refreshed.

I felt a tinge of sadness for Chuck. I knew he'd rather be here with his own sons than chaperoning someone else's kids on a home-repair work trip to Kentucky. The group had left from Ames the day before. When he found out we'd had dinner together, he would feel lonely.

We ate our meal on the deck, the early evening sky a bright blue, a breeze lightening the oppressiveness of the July humidity. Keegan sighed as he chewed his steak. "Perfect," he said. I glanced at him, worried about whether he was getting enough food and sleep as he marched through his frantic summer schedule. His constant workout for college soccer meant he was all muscle, but sometimes he had dark circles under his eyes. Tonight, though, he looked healthy.

Now I stole a look at Jesse, who leaned back from his plate. With a new degree in cinema studies, he hoped to find a job out west in film editing. But were film grads as plentiful there as were English majors around Iowa City?

I sighed. All of us going different directions.

And then they were gone: Jess to finish his last class project, Keegan to see his girlfriend. I stepped into the garage, holding the door open for Ginger. She eyed the mower as I filled it with gas. As I revved it up, she barked, hating the noise, but finally plopped down a few feet from me while I mowed. Every few minutes, she repositioned, staying parallel to the dreaded machine.

The oak trees swayed in the breeze. Near dusk, there was a faint crescent moon, and the western sunset, fluorescent mauve, cast a ring of pink on the eastern horizon. But I wasn't appreciating the color fest. I felt only blue about both sons leaving the state next month, sad that their home base would no longer be Iowa City. Would they even want to visit us in Ames? Would Ames ever feel like home to them?

And I was tired of mowing. The lawn was large, hilly, and slanted, the mower handle too high for my five-foot frame, no matter how I adjusted it. Chuck used to mow the backyard and I the flatter front and sides. But Pastor Chuck had been too busy tending to his shifting flocks.

John Wesley, an Englishman and founder of Methodism, set the pattern for the itinerancy system, believing preachers should keep moving so as not to become too comfortable with worldly possessions and ideas. Circuit riders, they were called— men who rode on horseback and preached in the open air. He and his brother Charles warned each other not to get married, possessed as they were with traveling around to save souls. In 1751, at the age of forty-eight, however, Wesley succumbed and married a widow named Mary Vazeille. She had four young children, but she left him in 1755, probably because the man was never home. Methodists leave this little deadbeat-dad fact out when they venerate Wesley. Too bad for Mary Vazeille that he couldn't have just bought a Harley for his midlife crisis instead of marrying her.

Not for the first time, I saluted the Catholics for not letting priests marry.

My thoughts turned to *Souls on Fire*, a book I'd read for my spirituality book group. In this collection of stories about legendary rabbis in Eastern Europe, Ellie Wiesel tells a story about a rabbi named Levi-Yitzhak of Berditchev, who regularly shook his fist at God for allowing suffering. The rabbi, Wiesel writes, did not hesitate "to remind God that He too had to ask forgiveness for the hardships He inflicted on His people." As I mowed, I tried to gain a sense of God's presence, but I felt nothing. I shook my fist. "I give up," I said out loud. "The house isn't selling, and I don't have the energy to even try to rent it. You 'called' my husband, presumably, and now your Methodists are moving us across the state. You've taken Grandma Cord, and we haven't even been able to let it register. Can't you help? We'll be out thousands of dollars if we don't sell this house. You worry about it. It's your damned mess."

After an hour, I slowly wheeled the lawn mower up the hill and into the garage, where I muttered, "And I might sue the Methodist Church, just to give you fair warning. And you know what? I would sue you if I could," I said, looking out at the sky. Ginger's ears flattened.

Someone called from the newspaper the next afternoon to see if I wanted to extend our rental ad another week. I said a polite no and hung up. I wasn't kidding the night before; it was God's mess now.

That evening, after dinner with friends, I returned home and noticed the light blinking on the answering machine. I punched the button and listened to a woman asking if our house was still for rent. I didn't want to answer. But the urgency in the caller's voice and that she was from out of town and staying at a hotel aroused my empathy. I could at least call her back to let her know the house was no longer available.

Her voice was young and vibrant. She pleaded. "I'm here from Alaska, and I'm trying to find a rental house in the Wickham Elementary School district. I have two children and I've been told that's the best. Is yours inside the Wickham boundary?"

I felt irritated, protective of the elementary school our sons attended in a less-affluent Coralville district. "Every school is great in Iowa City and Coralville," I said. "But, yes, we're in the Wickham district."

"I have to fly back tomorrow," she said. "May I see your house tonight?"

I hesitated, doubting it would lead to anything. But she was so far from home, and I certainly knew the uncertainty of being uprooted. I gave her the directions.

A striking woman in her thirties, Carol told me she had two young children and her husband was a physician. They wanted to rent while they looked to buy or build a larger house. She liked the way most of our windows faced southeast. "We're from Alaska and really sun-deprived," she said, laughing.

Wistful, I remembered my own excitement fourteen years earlier when my editing job at ACT brought us to Iowa City. My Iowa City. Home.

We settled on a monthly rental amount that would cover a little more than our mortgage. She agreed to have the lawn cared for and to allow the house to be shown to potential buyers beginning again in February. The lease would end in March so the house would be empty for the next selling season.

St. Joseph hadn't found us a buyer, but he had bought us some time. Maybe it helps to shake a fist at God once in a while.

CHAPTER 15

New Lives

2003

In March of 2003, on a plane from Iowa to San Francisco, I thought about how much I still missed a full house.

I missed our sons, now twenty-three and twenty and on adventures of their own. I missed their voices, their music, their messy rooms, their friends swooping in for impromptu meals. I missed the details invoked by their interests that lent sure, immediate purpose to my own life. I missed the way Chuck and I made a good team as parents, he cooking our dinners and encouraging Jess and Keegan to take risks, I coordinating their schedules and reminding them to do their homework.

I was never one of those relaxed, creative mothers who made their own baby food and nursed their babies past a year. "Earth mothers," we called them. I worried too much, especially during our boys' baby and toddler years. Even so, I was fascinated by our sons from the beginning. I liked reading them books and trying to answer their questions. I remember Jess, age three, grappling with the death of our cat. "But we don't die—the Kelseys don't die, right?" he asked.

I liked joining Keegan, age seven, on neighborhood walks in the evenings after he'd say, "Mom, let's go for a walk and talk about life." We'd ask each other questions like "What would you do with a million dollars?" and "What do you want to be when you grow up?" He wanted to be a scientist, he said, and make potions to save sick people. "Or if those medicines are already invented, I'll make formulas that will make the snow rise up to the windowsills."

I was grateful for my flexible teaching and freelancing schedule so I could drive our sons to soccer practices; I'd read in the car or grade papers until they finished. I liked doing their laundry. I liked teaching them responsibility by designating chores. I didn't even mind filling in for their paper route. I was honored when they asked for help on a school essay. I also liked setting their dental and doctor appointments, teaching them how to drive and diagnose car symptoms, helping them search for the right college. Sometimes I ached to have a few days by myself, but for the most part, I liked being depended upon. I enjoyed being a mother. I was served by serving our sons.

And so I missed our full house. As our plane neared San Francisco and Chuck, Keegan, and I waited to set our eyes on Jess, I turned back to the riddle I'd been pondering ever since he left for college five years earlier: How could we be us without all of us?

When he greeted us at the San Francisco airport, Jesse's sturdy frame was relaxed, his eyes serene. Chuck grabbed him in a bear hug. When I hugged him, seven long months after his move to San Francisco, I cried. He laughed gently and returned my strong hold.

He brimmed with quiet excitement about his audition the night before with a band adding a trombone, one of his specialties, to their horn section. "Alternative rock with a jazz influence," he said in his pleasant baritone as Keegan slung an arm around his older brother. I savored the sight of them together: Jess shorter and stockier, his hair dark and skin brown; Keegan taller, lighter, with fair skin and blond-brown hair. Both have their father's gorgeous eyes—large and heavily lashed—but Jesse's are milk chocolate, like Chuck's, and Keegan's blue-gray.

Jesse drove us across the bay bridge toward the house he shared with five roommates near Berkeley. "Let's see the Albany Bulb," he said. "It was a construction landfill peninsula; now it's an outdoor art gallery in the wild."

The windless early spring day was painted with a loaded brush—bright blue, yellow-green—and the air smelled fresh. As we walked a gravel path, tall birches with shedding trunks gave way to saplings and bushes. After half a mile Jess pointed to a large hunk of concrete swirled in rusted rebar. On the mound sat a life-sized ceramic skull glazed with muted pinks, yellows, and blues. Framed by bushes and tall grass, the sculpture was a barely visible suggestion of an expressionless man wrapped in a concrete blanket.

As he led us down the final stretch of path, Jess said, "About thirty years ago the city of Albany allowed a construction dump site here, but the operator illegally dumped plant debris, and it caused a bunch of methane fires." The city eventually abandoned the area. Plants and animals reclaimed the land, and a homeless community settled in, building shacks near the water. Artists began creating sculptures and paintings out of the dumped concrete and rebar and out of Styrofoam and other flotsam. His tone turned wistful: "Of course, there were complaints about the homeless people, so they were forced to leave. But the art has been left, at least for now."

A row of large paintings faced the bay, exposed to weather. The faint smell of fish rose from the water. Keegan aimed his camera at art painted on upright pieces of old dock and signed "Sniff." Jess told us that Sniff was a group of anonymous artists who met here on Saturdays to create together. We smiled at the colorful, burlesque representations of people and animals drinking and cavorting.

Along the bay was a bunker of concrete, rocks, and hunks of Styrofoam, large enough to accommodate six people. A poured-concrete stairway led to the flat roof with a view of the San Francisco skyline and the Golden Gate Bridge. I climbed the roof to luxuriate in the sun, the sixty-five-degree temperature, the fact that we wouldn't have to say goodbye to Jess for five days, and the murmurs of my family.

Jess was absorbed by a metal Icarus sculpture ten yards away. Friends his age were beginning graduate or medical school or landing jobs with shiny new business degrees. Always fond of the road less traveled, our son worked in a camera store developing film while he sought work in film editing and sound design and spent his spare time in places like this. I liked that he was managing to make ends meet even on an ascetic's income. I liked that he found this place and shared it with us on our first day.

Not many people from this area even knew about the Albany Bulb. I liked that our son knew.

The second day Jess suggested a drive to Muir Woods, north of San Francisco. The forest, relatively undisturbed for thousands of years, was now one of the last uncut stands of redwoods—a sanctuary. We stepped away from noise and into cool air rich with oxygen and humus. "The air is moister in here. For California, that is," I said, thinking about the humidity we'd face in Iowa over the summer.

Jess smiled. "Every time I come here, I feel lighter and my shoulders loosen up. Just breathe the air and you'll feel so relaxed." We climbed the Ocean View Trail and saw Douglas firs, maples, oaks, buckeyes, and redwoods that were 500, 800, even 1,000 years old, some 22 feet around and 370 feet high. Iowa's tallest oaks and cottonwoods are a quarter the height of these redwoods. I felt comfortably insignificant in this giant old forest that filtered the light into a hundred shades of green.

After an hour's climb we reached the top of the trail and sat on large rocks in a meadow. Now we could hear the incongruous noise of cars on a busy road above us. Jess casually pointed to the ocean in the distance, a horizontal glimmer of silver that I might have mistaken for a cloud. Keegan picked up a small rock and pocketed it—an echo of times we'd collected smooth Lake Michigan rocks north of Chicago and dimpled Lake Superior stones near Duluth. "For my boss," I heard him tell Jess.

Keegan had taken a semester's hiatus from college to decide where to transfer and to earn some money. He lived with us in Ames, but we barely saw him; he held two jobs from 4 a.m. to 5 p.m., five days a week, and visited his girlfriend in Wisconsin on weekends. Sleep-deprived and missing his independence, he found this purgatory difficult. "She has a rock collection and asked me to find some," he told his brother. "Stressed-out single mom with three kids."

As we descended the path, I breathed the thick air in gratitude. Jess had found sacred space in his new environment, and Keegan's spirit was still generous.

The third day we took in the San Francisco Museum of Modern Art, the SF MOMA. Jess was a talented sketcher, Keegan a photographer and sculptor. Chuck cooks and gardens; I write and paint. At art museums, we each gravitate to our interests. Jess and Chuck headed for the multimedia exhibits, Keegan to the photographs, and I to the paintings, anticipating a feast of modernism. Art triggers the same sense of awe for me that being in nature does. One nonrepresentational painting by Clyfford Still especially spoke to me: Burgundy and cranberry covered a large canvas, and then a small, jagged line of black. It was comforting to think that a man would create, at forty-seven—my age—such a mystical and luxurious painting. I sat for minutes on a bench, mesmerized by the painting's rich shimmer. It seemed to say, like Julian of Norwich, the mystic, "All shall be well and all shall be well and all manner of things shall be well."

Our dinner afterward at a tapas restaurant just around the corner held the aura of the movie *Babette's Feast*. Chuck, a tapas artist himself, had educated our family's palate for years. A continuous comfort through the busy years of raising our sons was having meals together. Our dining was always infused with graceful artistry, from twenty-minute meals to those made for extended family or friends over two days' time. Our sons learned early on to try new foods under the eye of the chef, who watched our reactions carefully. Jess and Keegan had picked up some of Chuck's culinary skills and appreciation for good food.

We ordered a round of drinks, some breads, and assorted olives and then a second round of more complicated dishes. The appreciation of the food flowed, but after a while, Keegan looked at his father and said, "It's great food, but I've had even better from you." Chuck's face turned sober, the way it does when the compliment means so much he can't answer. Then he made a toast: "To Jess and his new adventure, to Keegan and his next phase of school, and to all of us."

All would be well. Indeed, all was well.

The fourth day Jess went to work at the camera store and Keegan to Santa Barbara by bus to investigate a photography school. Though difficult, we respected that he didn't want our company as he had two years earlier during his first college search. Chuck and I packed and loaded the car for a twenty-four-hour trip, just the two of us, a little island of romance in the middle of the family vacation, just as we had taken semiannual

B&B getaways while the boys were growing up. The boys would likely appreciate the break from us as well.

We chose Sonoma County, a road a little less traveled than Napa Valley. We saw rolling, pastoral hills—echoes of southeast Iowa, except instead of corn and soybeans, the green, grassy fields were full of newly-leafed grapevines stretched across cables. We visited wineries around Sonoma, but Chuck became most animated at a little olive oil store outside the tiny village of Glenn Ellen. Inside, a woman described the four oils we could sample, each with a piece of bread. We dipped the breads, noted the differences, and then Chuck drank the remains of the samples—carried away in wine country. I smiled at my mate. That evening we feasted on crab cakes, sea bass, and beer at a lovely restaurant along the Sonoma town square. We walked back in the cool California air to a bed and breakfast, where we sat in the hot tub on the roof of the second floor, watching tree tops wave in the night breeze.

Even after months of our sons being gone and years of practicing our B&B getaways, it felt odd to be just the two of us together. Someone once told me, "It's easy to add a plate to the family table, but it's hard to take one away." I gazed at Chuck, who savored the hot swirling water. He'd always been more flexible, more accepting than me; I was having the tougher time missing the two plates. I smiled at him, asking him silently to bear with my sadness. He touched my hand.

The next morning—the fifth day—we lingered in our room at the inn, sipping coffee and reading the paper in bed. Fresh air wafted in an unscreened open window.

I said, "I don't want to say goodbye to Jess today." Chuck nodded but didn't respond. I didn't expect him to. What could he say? I set my cup on the nightstand, put on shorts and a shirt, and said I was going for a stroll. He nodded again, respecting my need to be alone.

I walked around the sleepy town square and thought about how dependent I became on our sons while they were growing up for my *raison d'etre*. It was ironic for someone who hadn't planned on having children. Our pregnancy with Jess came by surprise a year after I finished my bachelor's degree, and even Keegan was not entirely planned. As a feminist I embraced the idea that being a mother shouldn't preclude my desire to work outside the home. But to my surprise, motherhood was my most compelling vocation. And now I missed our full house.

I sighed and returned to the inn, where I met Chuck in the lobby for breakfast.

Our last day in San Francisco was unexpectedly light. Jess was sweet and funny, dancing a few steps down the sidewalks, leaping on benches, mimicking a laid-back California drawl. Chuck and I ate lunch with him in Berkeley—a golden time alone with him—and then the three of us drove across the bay into San Francisco. "You've got to see the ocean up close before you leave," he insisted. We drove to a thin strip of beach where it was cold and windy, the waves crashing onto the shore, the horizon a muted blue, turquoise, and violet.

From there we drove to Golden Gate Park and hiked up and down green hills and around a pond toward the beautiful, if slightly seedy, Japanese tea garden. We met Keegan, euphoric from the scenic train ride back along the coast from Santa Barbara. We drank overpriced tea served by girls in geisha dress, and we hiked the garden path, admiring the designs. After dinner and coffee in Chinatown, it was time to drive to the airport. Jess thanked us for coming. He returned our grasping hugs, but he was at ease. As we drove away, I was reassured by the spring in his step as he headed down Market Street toward the BART station for home or maybe to duck in a bar to hear some live music. Exploring his city.

On the way to the airport I thought about how each son was flourishing in his own way. Jess was living an adventure, playing trombone and guitar, experimenting with video and film. Keegan was looking for ways to develop his artistic side by transferring to an art or photography school.

Chuck and I, too, were exploring new avenues of creativity in Ames. Chuck was branching into some serious gardening. He was flourishing as an associate pastor, helping create an evening meal program for those in need. Food at First, staffed by volunteers from all over town, was growing popular.

I was in new writing territory—a novel. I loved my office in the parsonage with its second-floor deck built so craftily above the lower-level sun porch—the treehouse, we called it, because of the way branches framed it. In warm weather I edited at a rickety plastic green table, Ginger sleeping at my feet, the oak canopy swaying and whispering above. We'd sold our house, finally, in Iowa City, and Chuck had created a frame in our Ames backyard for the wooden swing we'd bought so many years earlier.

As I added all of it up in my head, I admitted that maybe I did know the answer to my riddle. Chuck, Jess, Keegan, and me—we were us and would always be us. Except for Keegan's brief hiatus from college, we didn't live together anymore, but we all shared a love of creating that transcended place.

Like the artists of the Albany Bulb, we were all making new lives out of old materials that had resided in our family all along—a love of art, nature, music, good food, and love itself.

CHAPTER 16

The Hero and the Hermit

2006

I EXPECTED RAMSHACKLE, BUT THIS WAS A NORTH WOODS palace. A high-ceilinged great-room with a stone fireplace and windows that revealed Lake Superior. Knotty pine walls with works of local women artists: watercolors and oils of the lake, trees, moose, and seagulls; *The Lady of the Lake* wall sculpture, plump and rounded, with a fish in her woven belly; a woman on the *What You See Is What You Get* quilt sitting cross-legged, unselfconscious, presiding on the high wall above the planked dining room table with wooden benches. Each of the four bedrooms—two on ground floor, two lofted—named after a writer: Amy Tan, Audre Lord, Barbara Kingsolver. Mine, the Julia Alvarez room.

Our bedrooms were sanctuaries: log-frame beds with locally made quilts, chests, nightstands, reading lamps, and towels supplied for us and cleaned three times a week. Little wicker baskets for transporting toiletries to the shower house or Jacuzzi room.

Our writing sheds were tiny log structures with slanted roofs sequestered among birches just 100 feet from the lake. Mine was named after Adrienne Rich. The shed held a comfortable, adjustable office chair, with a rocking chair and shelves in opposite corners. A pine shelf for a desk lined a wall with two large windows that looked out at Lake Superior. The Divine Ms. S, I called her, watching her diva moods, one day benevolent indigo against light blue sky; the next, steel gray and white-capped against gunflint ceiling.

JUNE 2006   I was in the North Woods of Minnesota, near Lutsen, living in a cabin along Lake Superior. The writing gods had smiled upon me; I was selected for a three-week writers' retreat at a place called Norcroft. Writer and founder Joan Drury had saved the souls of more than six hundred women like me, providing time, quiet, rooms of our own, and eight-by-eight sheds in which to write. I lived with three other women in the lodge built in the 1940s and remodeled after Joan bought it in the early 1990s.

From my shed I could dimly hear cars and trucks behind me on Highway 61. When I opened the generous windows, the dominant sounds were lapping waves, birdsong, rustling birch leaves, the soft hiss of pine boughs filtering wind.

My first day in my shed I was so in awe of the view, I couldn't write.

After ten days, I could still think only in terms of cliché: I was in heaven, living a dream, a writer's trance. After coffee and breakfast, I showered each morning, then padded fifty feet to my writing shed. I wrote all morning, stopping for tea and a snack halfway through. Kay, the caretaker, stocked the pantry with special teas, walnuts and pumpkin seeds, craisins, fresh fruit. I fixed my lunch, nodding and smiling to my cabin mates. We could not speak to each other until 4:00 p.m. I ate at the dining room table, gazing at the lake, or walked down to the gazebo just above the rocky shore.

After lunch I read or took a short nap, letting my body relax out of its writer's pose, and then I walked back to my shed, inhaling the pungent, sweet scent of pine resin and the earthy moistness of wildflowers and other plants. I crossed a wooden footbridge and said hello to the little brook that flowed down to the lake. Then back to the shed until 4:00, when I stretched, shut off the laptop, stepped lightly back to the cabin, and donned sweat clothes.

Then I would jog a few miles or hike an hour on the Superior Hiking Trail, the 240-mile path that stretches along the ridgeline adjacent to Lake Superior from Duluth to the Canadian border. I admired the wildflowers: Virginia bluebells, prominent the first week, then giving way to trillium—canopied plants with orchidlike blossoms underneath and ubiquitous as the mayapples back home in mid-May. I saw wood anemone—smaller versions of the meadow anemone back home—and wild strawberry plants in blossom. For the first time I saw painted Indians—green flowers tipped by a cosmic artist's brush with orange-red nature paint. They looked so fake, I laughed.

Relieved not to have to make conversation during the day, I could go about my work without giving a single thought to someone else's needs. By the end of my first week, this steady work was having an effect: I was finally thinking of myself as a Writer with a capital W.

And with my life so well-balanced now between work and play, I was also definitely feeling Alive with a capital A. And still no Prozac necessary, thank you.

I thought back fourteen years to when Chuck decided to be a minister. In the midst of all that turmoil, my inner voice was telling me, "Support him. You, too, will find your calling."

I had found it.

Evenings Betsey, Martha, Kara, and I talked and cooked together, then laughed while we ate stir-fry, salads, or grilled chicken at the long wooden table. We cleaned up, then returned to our sheds or hiked another leg of the Superior Trial. After dark we lit a fire in the lodge, invisibly built by Kay during the day, and settled on the couch and overstuffed chairs to read from our day's work.

Kara, our New Yorker and twenty-six-year-old youngster, treated us to acts from her play about a Gulf War vet. Or she read bits from a new piece—a novel that, to her surprise, had emerged her second day. We teased that her creative self was doing pirouettes for her attention now that she had time away from a demanding editing job.

Martha, a therapist in her fifties from Minneapolis, read about her "before" and "after" life since suffering a head injury in a car accident. Despite her serious topic, Martha's eyes lit up as she read, now connected with the writing self that had long been dormant.

Betsey, sixty-one and a dancer from New Jersey but a New Englander at heart, read from her manuscript about living in a girls' home for unwed mothers and the unexpectedly warm community of young girls and supportive social workers. We knew she had given up her baby and adopted a son years later. As she read, we shared the ambivalence of her seventeen-year-old self about having to make the decision as she neared labor.

Betsey and Kara's readings were infused with the voices and mannerisms of their characters. Betsey became a pregnant adolescent dancer, Kara a tired vet.

These comrades listened to drafts of the early chapters of this book. It was gratifying to hear them laugh in the right places and even in parts I didn't expect. When I was worried a passage was too whiny, they reassured me. "No, these are real issues; I would feel that way too." With this gift of a live audience, I could hear what needed to be cut and what needed smoothing.

And what worked.

As I drafted scenes of Jesse and Keegan, I could see them as young boys and hear their high-pitched voices. This didn't bring back the empty nest sadness and grief I experienced for so long after they left home. Instead, writing about them completed the experiences, allowing me to appreciate them even more deeply.

Suspended from my usual life in Ames, I had time to reflect on it. I still missed Iowa City, but Ames was growing on me. I'd given myself permission to attend the Unitarian Fellowship, where other attendees shared my agnosticism and a love of nature. Tall sanctuary windows revealed the trees and purple coneflowers outdoors. Songs and talks—not sermons—often nodded to nature's beauty and the grace and wisdom to be gained from the natural. In a small spirituality group of fifteen women, I found others who looked for the common threads in diverse religions, who sometimes saw glimpses of that mystical, invisible river that I saw in many spiritual traditions. The Unitarians were a good tribe for me. Neither Chuck nor his congregation seemed to object.

Howard would have been proud.

I had fallen in love with the house too—the parsonage—room by room. First, my office, and then the second-floor deck. Chuck and I had learned to enjoy the rituals of being just-a-twosome again, carrying our evening meals up to the treehouse, toasting to each other with a glass of wine. "To the Pastard," I would say, a term of endearment he understood to mean "I'll never love being a minister's wife, but I love you." In reply, he would say, "To the perfect minister's wife," which I knew to mean "Don't ever stop being irreverent."

I loved our bedroom with its large windows inviting sun from the south and west. The sunny glassed-in porch downstairs lined with plants. The dining room and living room, where soon

I would serve snacks to the church trustees as they inspected the house, which they did annually.

Yes, I loved this house where our sons and their girlfriends gathered, making it feel like home. A place where my parents, in-laws, our siblings and their families converged for holiday meals.

Indeed, the greatest gift of Ames was the growing closeness with our extended families, especially as our parents began to face health challenges. My dad's emphysema had worsened, but he stoically trekked out with his oxygen tank. Mom had experienced several fractured vertebrae. They'd moved to the Des Moines area to be closer to my brother, sister, and me. Living in Ames we were now just an hour away from Chuck's parents. His father had bypass surgery just after our move to Ames. His mother was about to undergo a knee replacement.

I liked my growing circle of friendships in Ames—the Unitarians and a dear friend, Kelly, who sketched with me at the outdoor arboretum. "Better than church," we agreed, breathing deeply under oak trees as our watercolor brushes flew. Katie, loyal running buddy, and other runners in a club training for a half-marathon. Bob and Deb, old friends from Iowa Falls who had just moved to town. Their excitement about living in a university town helped me see Ames with even more appreciative eyes.

More than anything, I was finally getting Chuck and me, finally understanding who we were, individually and together. I knew why we had conflicts and why we stayed together. I was on to us.

We were the Hero and the Hermit.

Betsey had loaned me Caroline Myss's book *Sacred Contracts*, and in the late evenings, I snuggled in bed and read. Myss joins a longtime dialogue begun by Carl Jung about archetypes. Jung believed all souls were connected by what he called the collective unconscious, a sum of all the experiences that humans have had over time. He believed that out of the collective unconscious emerge various psychological patterns of behavior that manifest in dreams, ideas, and stories as characters with particular personalities.

He called these characters archetypes and described some of them: the Mother, the Trickster, the King, the Servant. Jung felt these archetypes undergirded our personalities and actions. Myss suggests that each of us has our own constellation of key archetypes. She believes that looking at our constellations can help us with problems or challenges, liberating us from the limitations of our thoughts and feelings.

In my late-night reading, I quickly identified what I thought were our dominant archetypes. Chuck was the Hero, always on a quest to help others. His flexibility, ability to size up the situation at hand—especially in crisis—his good humor, and his love of taking risks are all essential heroic qualities. In our younger days he took physical risks that scared, angered, and amazed me—doing Evel Knievel stunts on his Harleys, walking too close to the edge of cliffs, scrambling up his parents' steep roof to patch a leak, sending four-year-old Jess off to Grandma's across the quarter-mile pasture.

As we had grown older, his risk-taking had become more psychological—like agreeing to start a new church in Iowa City in spite of his clergy peers warning him he was being set up to fail with such poor initial funding from the conference. But he'd forged ahead confidently, and the church eventually stabilized.

Myss says, "The Self emerges as the Hero faces physical and internal obstacles, confronting the survival fear that would compromise his journey of empowerment and conquering the forces arrayed against him. The Hero then returns to the tribe with something of great value to all." And, yes, gets to enjoy that kowtowing when he comes back with the booty.

I was not a Hero. "The Hermit," Myss writes, "withdraws from others to pursue a solitary life," sometimes for spiritual purposes, à la the Mystic (another archetype), sometimes to make contact with the beauty of life and nature—à la Henry David Thoreau or Emily Dickinson, sometimes out of fear of what others think—à la me on my worst days.

I saw myself in all these facets of the hermit's personality. Myss helped me see that I was simply following my natural tendencies. I withdrew occasionally, not wanting to be distracted by what others might think of me. But most of the time now I was in that Thoreau-Dickinson camp, connecting with beauty through nature, jogging, writing, reading, and creating art. Occasionally I even reached that mystical realm of transcendence of the ordinary, of union with the divine—that invisible river. Of the Mystic, Myss says, "Many want to believe that they have mystical inclinations yet underestimate how arduous the genuine mystical path is." While the lives of the world's great mystics have often included extraordinary states of consciousness, she says, they also contain hard work, routines that most would consider mundane, and physical or spiritual suffering.

Amen, sister. I knew about the spiritual suffering. I realized each archetype must have its drawbacks, but all I could do was speak for my own: It can be a real challenge to be a hermit-mystic when you're married to a person whose work thrusts you into the public sphere. Even now, as I thought about plunging back into my hero's church world back in Ames, I could feel my body almost physically bracing for its chaos.

Yet I felt ready to return now that I got us. Chuck needed to be the Hero; I needed to be the Hermit. It was as simple as that. He was the active; I was the contemplative. He needed my steady, routine presence to come home to; after all, didn't I hear the desperate loneliness in his voice when I called home? He missed me.

Yes, I would probably always hate the unpredictability of his schedule and the way church meetings and parishioners' needs often trumped mine. And I was jealous, sometimes, of the hero's accolades, which do not often come the Hermit's way. On the other hand, he had to endure my remoteness when I was wrapped up in a piece of writing. Or the way I can be irritable if I need time alone.

We were who we were. No more fighting it. It was time to get down to business and enjoy the rest of our lovely, blessed lives together.

Monday morning of my second week at Norcroft, I stepped into the kitchen in my bare feet and fuzzy pink and blue robe. Betsey, her hair pulled back into a dancer's bun, was rustling in the refrigerator. A pattern had emerged. She and I had become the engineers of the food, each of us needing a plan for the evening before we could begin our day's work. She wrote a note to us all while I made my coffee: "Shall we have stir-fry tonight with vegetables and tofu?" I nodded, then scribbled on another piece of paper: "We are such mothers!" She smiled. I scribbled again. "Did you choose the 'Mother' as one of your archetypes? I think you should!"

Betsey wrote, "I guess I thought since I gave up my daughter,

I didn't qualify for the 'Mother' archetype." Her gorgeous eyes were sad. I shook my head and waved a finger at her.

I poured my coffee and walked back to my bedroom, thinking about how hard it would be to have birthed a child who now would be forty-three years old, just a few years younger than me. To have to wonder where she was or if she was still alive. To have to hope that she would get curious enough to make contact. Betsey had no rights to contact her daughter; she wasn't even sure if her daughter knew she was adopted. Every time she moved, she updated the adoption agency's records, hoping her daughter would initiate a connection. I thought of my own long difficulties in letting Jesse and Keegan go. Betsey and I were linked in this way—we just had to let go differently and at different times. I scribbled a note in my room. "Letting a child go is one of the criteria for being a mother."

I returned to the kitchen, where Betsey was cutting strawberries to put on her cereal. I handed her the note. She read it and put her hand over her heart. She dropped her hands and then composed herself, folding the note and putting it in her shirt pocket. She smiled at me, raising her arms for a hug. We held each other tightly, then stepped away, smiling.

With a written sentence, I had been of service to someone—my Hermit briefly turned Mystic.

Early Saturday afternoon at the end of my second week at Norcroft, it was almost time for Chuck to arrive for a twenty-four-hour visit. He had taken this weekend off, including Sunday—a rare treat these days. The drive was about nine hours, but he planned to arrive around 2:00. I stewed about the condition of our old Plymouth Voyager minivan with 200,000 miles.

In my shed around 1:00 p.m., I stood up from the laptop and stretched. Lake Superior was royal blue near the horizon, teal in the middle, gray in the strip closest to shore, and a little choppy. But it was sunny, at least, so maybe we'd have good weather in Grand Marais, twenty miles north. I'd booked a motel. No visitors were allowed at Norcroft except for short tours on Saturdays.

I walked from my shed to the cabin to pour one more cup of coffee, intending to write another half hour. I crossed the little wooden footbridge, missing the sound of the gurgling brook, nearly dry since there had been no rain for several days. From the kitchen I heard a motorcycle pull up. Peeking out the window, I saw Kay emerging from her caretaker's cabin. Her new boyfriend, I decided. I picked up my cup and prepared to head back to my lovely little shed.

The door opened to the laundry room, and I heard steps coming through the kitchen. "He's here," Kay said.

"Huh?"

"He's here. Your husband."

"The guy on the bike? I thought that was your new boyfriend!"

"Nope, it's your husband," said Kay, smiling.

I ran outside the cabin to the little parking lot. There was Chuck, leaning against a motorcycle, just like in his old Harley days. Instead of the James Dean cool he used to exude, he was grinning like Goofy. He opened his arms to me in his old black leather jacket. It was stretched tightly across his chest and hit him above the waist now.

My Hero in a miniature jacket. I giggled.

He grinned and grabbed me tightly. "I rented the bike in Ames. Jess and Keeg knew about this, but I told them to keep it quiet. I figured you'd worry too much."

"You're damned right."

"And your mom tried to talk me out of it. She said, 'Oh, Charlie, be careful.'"

I smirked at my husband who likes to make my mother worry. Part of a Hero's makeup: How can a Hero be a Hero if people don't worry?

"I'll bet she did," I said, willing my voice to stay calm, but thinking about how I told Betsey she could use my car to drive to Grand Marais to see the solstice pageant since I thought we'd have the van. Should I tell her she couldn't have the car now? I didn't want to ride that bike up there, thinking of all the antics he used to pull. I stalled for time to think. "Want the grand tour?"

"Sure."

He took my hand in his. We walked down to the lake, and I showed him the gazebo. Inside, we kissed, and I felt uncertain. This was a women's-only retreat; would his yang energy disturb all the yin? We walked back up to the cabin, and I showed him my room, then we walked the little path to my shed.

"Wow," he said. "I feel like I shouldn't be in here—like it's your private sanctuary. You want one of these at home?"

I knew he'd build one in a day if I said yes. "No, I love my office at the parsonage."

Stepping toward the cabin again, I continued stewing about how to get to Grand Marais, but as we entered my bedroom, I took a big breath and said, "Do you have two helmets for that beast?"

"You want to ride it?"

"Yep. Because I told Betsey she could use the car."

We took my suitcase outside and stuffed it into one of the Harley's storage compartments.

Chuck handed me his helmet.

"Nope," I said. "You wear it."

"Nope. You."

"Nope, I insist. You."

He opened a storage compartment and started putting the helmet inside.

"Okay, okay," I said, grabbing the helmet.

"I figured there'd be no way you'd ride, so I didn't bring two," he said. "Hey, listen to this." He punched a CD player, and I heard the drum and heavy metal intro to "Born to Be Wild." I laughed.

"Jess mixed a CD of biking music for me." Chuck pulled out the CD and showed me the cover: Jess had created a cartoon of his dad standing on top of a motorcycle. I laughed.

He folded down my foot pegs, I jumped on behind him, and we headed up Highway 61—no racing, no swerving, no bellowing Harley acceleration, nothing that I expected might resurface from the past. Nothing but a smooth, sixty-miles-per-hour ride. I began to relax. My husband knew me, now, and the knowing me had become more important than the showboating.

I leaned into Chuck, lifting my hands from the passenger grips and wrapping my arms around him. He held my hands with one hand, wiggling his back to show his happiness, just like in the old days. I lay my helmet on his shoulder, and he snuggled his head back against my helmet. We headed north toward Grand Marais, basalt volcanic cliffs on our left, the Divine Ms. S. winking on our right.

CHAPTER 17

Exile

2007–12

IN MAY OF 2007, FIVE YEARS AFTER OUR MOVE TO AMES, the Iowa Methodist Bishop and his cabinet announced Chuck's appointment July 1 to DeWitt, a small town of 5,000, three hours away on Highway 30, on the eastern edge of the state.

In the hinterlands.

Neither of us wanted to go, but I was in the middle of a health crisis that included unexplained weight loss and other worrisome symptoms. My physician was running tests to rule out ovarian cancer. This was not the time to give up our health insurance provided by Chuck's job. I, the reluctant minister's wife, was now the reason my husband remained in ministry.

The parsonage in DeWitt was dark, unlike the sun-filled house in Ames. If I ventured out to the town's tiny coffee shop to work at my laptop, Chuck would tell me later that parishioners had reported spotting me as if I were a zoo animal on the loose.

On Sunday mornings they quizzed me—aggressively, it seemed—about my writing projects and where I would be traveling next for my work. If I missed church, I faced "We missed you's" that sounded accusing.

DeWitt was a stranger with prying eyes.

It was plain and flat except near the golf course and adjoining upscale housing development. When it rained hard, a creek in the only park in town overflowed, leaving the smell of mud and bird feces. With no university town accoutrements—lectures, readings, bookstores—I felt adrift.

Living in DeWitt was an exile of Babylonian proportions.

In *Burmese Days*, George Orwell wrote about the "devilishly difficult to explain" nature of exile:

> [It is a] pain that is all but nameless. Blessed are those who are stricken only with classifiable diseases! Blessed are the poor, the sick, the crossed in love, for at least other people know what is the matter with them and will listen to their belly-achings with sympathy. But who that has not suffered it understands the pain of exile?

I tried not to speak of my belly-achings to the people of DeWitt. Old friends and relatives told me to "Bloom where you're planted," their advice wise and practical but of little comfort. The reality is that we do grow more vigorously in some places than in others. We fall for places just like we fall for our mates. It had been love at first sight with Iowa City and me, and even Ames had become a good friend. But now, DeWitt. How would I survive DeWitt?

One day soon after our move, Ginger sprawled in the backyard of the rambling brick ranch parsonage. As she panted in the warm sun, I picked up some smooth landscaping stones clustered around the foundation. I made three small piles on the side of each step to the kitchen door. One cairn was for Iowa City—still Home-with-a-capital-H. Another represented Ames and its unexpected blessings. The third and smallest was little DeWitt.

I prayed. Dear Big Busy God who will be watching over Chuck and his new flock, will you ask some quiet little god to watch over me, living this unwanted public life in a very small fishbowl?

I took a few deep breaths. I am home. I have arrived, I told myself. It was a phrase I'd picked up from a book by Buddhist monk Thich Nhat Hanh.

But my stomach felt unsettled.

I would need the Buddha here.

Help me, Buddha.

I would need Jesus here too. Even though right then I hated the Methodist Church and John Wesley and the Methodist itinerancy and this dark house and this little town.

Lord Jesus Christ, have mercy on me.

I plugged away at my freelancing business with frequent travels to colleges out of state to gather research for writing marketing publications. Chuck and I exercised at the small fitness center. After a surgery, my health returned to normal. Thankfully, there was no cancer, but the homesickness lingered.

I'd read books about mindfulness, meditation, and Buddhism and decided a meditation practice might help me cope. I began driving seventy miles to Iowa City two Wednesdays a month to sit with a small Buddhist sangha at the old Unitarian Church near downtown. Each time, the group of ten or twelve meditated silently for thirty minutes, then spent an hour discussing an excerpt of writing by authors such as Thich Nhat Hanh and Pema Chödrön. During meditation I learned to watch my thoughts and feelings come and go with awareness, compassion, and nonjudgment.

I realized how utterly gripped I'd been by my likes and dislikes. Graspings and aversions, Buddhists call them—two major causes of suffering. With fascination I watched my thoughts come and go: I didn't want to live in such a small town; I wanted to return to Iowa City, or to Ames, or to anywhere more aesthetically and intellectually pleasing.

I wanted to be less lonely, more connected. Yet I didn't want to be too connected to the people of DeWitt. Superstitiously, I reasoned if I became too attached, I might get stuck there, grow old there. Wither and die there.

I was getting it: The grasping for Home was triggering my suffering. "What fires together wires together," neuroscientists say, meaning that when we ruminate over negative thoughts, our brains develop neuronal tracks to which the brain defaults, especially when under stress. I began to see that my thinking patterns were affecting not just me but also Chuck; and not just Chuck but also my family and friends back in Ames and Des Moines and Iowa City who knew I was in distress and frequently called to check on me. My refusal to warm up to DeWitt also surely affected the good, hospitable, amiable people there as well.

Dukkha, the Buddhists call it—that anxiety we experience when we are fixated, trancelike, on our graspings and aversions. Thich Nhat Hanh tells us to bring to ourselves the utmost compassion when we are aware of our dukkha. We are to tell ourselves, "Dear One, I'm here for you." Watching my thoughts and feelings, I saw the layers of suffering—not only the grief of leaving family and friends but also a layer of shame for carrying the grief.

I saw self-judgment. What was wrong with me that I couldn't turn it off? Yes, I loved Iowa City, but really, why couldn't I bloom where planted just for now? And why in the world had I left my community college teaching job with good benefits, making myself so financially vulnerable to wherever the Mighty Bishop and his Almighty Cabinet deemed we should live?

I began to offer compassion inward. "Dear One, I am here for you," I told myself, putting my hand over my heart as Thich Nhat Hanh recommended.

One time I asked the sangha, "Do you ever get to the point where your issues don't bother you anymore?"

Charity, one of the elders, smiled. "They just become irrelevant."

Miriam said, "When I am aware that my mind is getting triggered by one of my hot buttons, I say to myself, 'Oh, there's my stuff.'" She smiled and everyone laughed.

Another explained the Buddhist concept of the two arrows of suffering. "The first arrow is the external event that causes suffering. We have no control over that," he said. "The second arrow is the suffering we add with our thoughts. That layer we do have some control over. We can accept our thoughts with compassion, but we also can learn to let go of them. 'Dropping the storyline,' it's called," he said. "By dropping the narrative of what we want or don't want, even for just a few minutes, we can remove the second arrow of suffering and reduce the pain."

Each time, I soaked up the discussion. Then, under the night sky, I drove the 70 miles back to DeWitt, the town's dismal plainness stabbing my heart, triggering that desperate wanting to go Home.

Oh, there's my stuff. Dear One, I'm here for you. I know this is hard. But no need to grasp. In time, we'll get this figured out. For now, let's try dropping the story.

Breathe, Suzanne, breathe.

Lord Jesus Christ, have mercy.

Slowly, I made myself turn from the question of what I wanted from life to what did life want from me while I was in DeWitt? Chuck's parishioners seemed to want a "How's your family?" and a willingness to listen to them talk about their lives after the Sunday morning services. Eighty-something Lois wanted us to have an occasional dinner with her family so they would know us when Chuck officiated at her funeral. "I expect to pass while you're in DeWitt," she said, giving Chuck a stern grin. "And you'd better not leave until I do." As I got to know the congregants, I began to trust that their interest in my work and comings and goings was genuine.

Freelance writing opportunities came out of nowhere. A regional magazine editor contacted me, asking me for writing samples, which led to multiple assignments. The University of Iowa made room for me as an online instructor. Rose Frantzen, an up-and-coming *alla prima* artist from nearby Maquoketa, asked me to help her write a book for an upcoming exhibit at the Smithsonian National Portrait Gallery in D.C. *Portrait of Maquoketa* would feature 180 head-and-shoulders portraits of Frantzen's fellow Maquoketans. I savored the months of working on the book with Rose and her husband, Charles Morris. Then Chuck and I ventured to D.C. to join Rose and Chuck and dozens of their townspeople for the opening to the exhibit. I'll never forget their collective joy as they stood in front of their own portraits on the hallowed walls of the National Portrait Gallery.

I co-led an adult study group with Becki at the church on Sunday mornings and enjoyed planning with her over lunches. Several women from the study began meeting on Wednesday evenings for wine and dinner—Wednesday Wine Women, or WWW, we called ourselves. One evening Sheri drove us to the local pizza joint. On the way home, Patti surveyed Main Street and said fondly, "My little DeWitt."

"Yeah. Little DeFreaking DeWitt," I said. My private nickname had spilled out of my mouth. I held my breath.

They laughed heartily. Our weekly levity began to infuse normalcy, even in the hinterlands.

Eventually, I moved the stones of the three cairns into one large one, just for DeWitt. A squirrel knocked it down almost daily. Each time I rebuilt it, I reviewed what I was learning.

The Buddha taught that attachment to anyone or anything or any place is futile because nothing ever stays the same. Change is the only constant. All is impermanent.

For many years I witnessed this law of impermanence during my daily walks with Ginger in the woods near the Coralville Reservoir, then the postage stamp prairie on the edge of Ames, and the prairie in Scott County Park, north of DeWitt. Bloodroot pushes out of the ground in April like old, gnarled palms that turn youthful and flat as they rise, then old and leathery as spring progresses. Sweet Williams release their aromatic lilac scent for a few days in May, and then the smells turn musky and fade. Purple coneflowers bloom in June like they are forever, then pass the baton to their yellow cousins. In the fall a deer carcass gets picked over by hungry, cawing ravens; a hawk flies over with a screaming mouse in its talons. Canadian geese honk southward and then north again, leaving the old and sick behind.

All of this without a single complaint on anyone's part.

Before her last days in DeWitt, even dear Ginger silently accepted her own impermanence as her eyes turned milky and her joints turned stiff. Toward the end, she chased squirrels only in her dreams with yips and twitching paws.

If you let go a little, you'll have a little peace, the Buddhists say. If you let go a lot, you'll have a lot of peace. If you let go completely, you'll have complete peace. Mahusukha, the Great Happiness, the great release. Nature knows it and Ginger knew it.

I learned it, too, during the years of resisting our emptying nest and then finally accepting it and learning to love those precious times with our adult sons and, now, with their mates and our grandsons.

My dad had learned about letting go with his stoic acceptance of emphysema's progression and his eventual death. More recently, Chuck's mother, after receiving a stage-four pancreatic cancer diagnosis modeled how it can go: You get the report, and then you begin the process of letting go without giving up. No struggling necessary. Just accept the what-is. Don't give up living and laughing, but when it's time, let go. Chuck's father also showed us from the nursing home; even with dementia, he kept his gentle sense of humor to the very end.

Impermanence. Acceptance. Letting go.

I thought of these lessons almost daily as I restacked the cairn.

CHAPTER 18

The Privilege of a Lifetime

2012–14

BY THE FALL OF 2012, SAME-SEX MARRIAGES WERE LEGAL in Iowa, and Chuck agreed to officiate at a wedding for two good friends. He knew doing so was a risk to his credentials. Though Methodists used the slogan "Open Hearts, Open Doors," their doors were closed to clergy performing same-sex marriages. Not one to hide the truth, Chuck told his district superintendent about the wedding. Soon after, upper-level administrators called him to the headquarters in Des Moines, telling him a letter of reprimand had been placed in his file. "In other words, you've been spanked," I said upon his return home. My sober husband nodded. If he repeated the "offense," he could lose his job.

Meanwhile, Chuck had been in conversation with state leaders of the United Church of Christ (UCC), a progressive denomination that allows individual churches to decide whether their clergy can officiate same-sex marriages. In October 2012, a state UCC board enthusiastically approved funding for Chuck to start a new church in the Iowa City/Coralville area. They projected enough funding from state, national, and private sources to cover Chuck's salary and benefits as well as marketing and rental costs for two years—long enough, we thought, to establish a financially independent congregation.

The exile was over. We were going Home.

As it turns out, you really can go home again. You can resume walks with old friends in green spaces all around the city, and you can make new wonderful and interesting friends. Only an echo remains of the long, existential loneliness. It keeps you sensitive to others new to the community who are waiting for signs of welcome.

Yes, you really can go home again.

You just might not be able to stay.

Six months after our return to Iowa City, we learned that the rest of the expected two years' worth of funding had run out or not materialized. For many months we limped along on my earnings, our savings, and the generous donations of family and friends as Chuck continued to grow Journey UCC, a unique community of around fifty people, without funds for marketing or rental space. Finally and unwillingly, after eighteen months of struggle, he started applying for other jobs.

Meanwhile, Whispery Mary passed away the Friday after Thanksgiving 2014. Chuck and I called her that, privately and lovingly, to distinguish her from two other Marys in the congregation.

Her family called Chuck on Thanksgiving, just as our full house was winding down for bedtime. Her brother had done an internet search for Journey Church, he said, and he was surprised and relieved when Chuck answered his phone. Mary had been life-flighted by helicopter from northeast Iowa to the University of Iowa surgical intensive care unit after a car-train accident the night before. She had already coded once, the brother said, and the family might have to decide whether to remove life support. He was sorry—he knew Chuck was probably having time with family, Thanksgiving Day and all—but could Chuck come to the hospital?

Of course, Chuck said. We'd had a full condo since Sunday— Jess and his wife, Melanie, and our two young grandsons from California; Keegan from New York and his girlfriend, Natasha, from San Francisco. On Thanksgiving Day, we were joined by my mother, our siblings and their mates, and a niece for a day of food, games, laughter, conversation, and outdoor play with the little ones in the scant layer of new snow.

We'd said our goodbyes to our extended family and the rest of us were ready for bed. Except for Chuck and me, the house would empty out the next morning. The timing of the call was so in tune with Mary's quiet, self-effacing character. She'd tucked herself sweetly and unobtrusively into the church and into our lives during the time we'd known her. Now, in her dying, it was no different.

Chuck returned from the hospital about 1:30 a.m. In our bedroom while the rest of the family slumbered in theirs, he told me Mary had been on her way to spend Thanksgiving with her daughters, but she'd gotten lost. It was a common theme, her family told Chuck; she'd always been directionally challenged, and they were accustomed to her showing up hours late. Somehow Mary wound up miles off her path, stuck on a railroad track, and in the path of an oncoming train.

The physicians did everything they could to save her, but it wasn't enough. The family had to decide whether to remove life support. Her organs were dying, the surgeon told the daughters, but one of them didn't want to let go. She needed to see with her own eyes, Chuck related, so he accompanied her to Mary's bedside, where the surgeon grimly removed the sheet on Mary's body and showed her the injuries. The rest of the family waited outside the room while the daughter registered the reality. Chuck stood stoically and gently, I was sure, at her side. Over the years many families had told me how helpful he is during a crisis.

We didn't know Mary well. She'd been a social worker for the university for many years but was now retired and in her early sixties. She had thick, kinky-curly blonde hair and a radiant smile. She had wrestled for some time with physical pain and tended to whisper and mumble when she talked. But for about a year, even when her foot was in a boot because of a painful bunion surgery, she'd made her way with determination most Sundays to Journey Church. She also attended the Wednesday evening Theology Brewed sessions for casual conversation with others over coffee or beer.

I didn't usually attend Theology Brewed but happened to be there the week before Thanksgiving. Mary sat to my left that night. She said a few things that I didn't quite pick up, but someone brought up the idea of sacred space, and Mary said so clearly and quietly, "This church is sacred space to me."

By this time, two years into Journey, the church wasn't sacred to me so much as complicated and uncomfortable because of the fiscal cliff Chuck and I faced. His work with the church was meaningful, there was no question, and I felt a part of the church because of the progressive thinking of the small congregation. But beginning in just one or two months, it would officially become a hobby, not a source of income, with no more paychecks for Chuck because of the unexpected, early withdrawal of support from the state and national UCC entities. As far as I could see, Journey was all washed up. But my husband wasn't admitting it, and now there was a silent, growing rift between us because of it.

That night I blinked myself out of my handwringing about our finances and focused on what Mary had said. The church was sacred space for her. And others around the circle had nodded. Journey was serving its intended purpose, at least for some.

Mary died the Friday after Thanksgiving, just hours after life support was removed. Chuck met with the family on Saturday to discuss the preparation for the memorial to be held Sunday afternoon.

I skipped the regular Sunday morning church service, grateful but tired after the six days of people packed into our small condo, yet also discontent, newly separated again from our dear family. Our grandsons were growing up so fast, yet we didn't see them enough, and right now we could not even afford to visit them in California.

Not wanting to dwell on these grasping thoughts, I turned to the Internet for spiritual food—to Daily Word, a service of the Unity Church that offers inspirational readings each day. Serendipitously, the message, "Hearing the Whisper," stated that there is "beauty and power when we listen to the whisper"— that still, small voice within each of us that speaks the truth and whispers assurances even when the "more insistent voices" in our heads deliver messages that make us anxious or afraid.

I thought of Mary's whispers. And then I called upon her, that morning, to help me hear my own truths whispering inside of me. To help me deal with my discontent, my darkness.

It had been a while since I'd felt connected to that voice, or what I'd come to call my Intuition-with-a-capital-I. I'd been so bound up in worry about our crumbling finances. I asked, *What is my truth this morning?*

"Go to Trueblood," Intuition piped up. It was a feeling inside my heart—not a voice, just a felt sense.

I looked outside. The willows outside the condo swayed like feathers in the wind. My iPhone said twenty degrees but it would feel like five degrees because of the wind chill. I donned my jeans and heavy down coat and drove a few miles to the Terry Trueblood Recreation Area, a former sand and gravel quarry, now ninety-five-acre lake with a walking trail through woods and restored prairie.

I walked the wooded side first, gazing at the frozen lake on that end. Along the second mile by the prairie, the lake water was open and choppy with the sharp wind. Hundreds of Canadian geese and wood ducks bobbed in the water. Just a little blue peeked through the gray sky. I kept my hood pulled close to my hat and listened to the Canadians honk, their white spots in sharp contrast to the gray sky and slate water.

As I neared the parking lot, sun and blue sky emerged from the clouds. Suddenly, the wavy waters gleamed like roiling silver. Sparkling. Magical. Transcendent.

"Remember that nature is your church, your sacred space," Intuition whispered. "That's how it's always been, and that's how it will always be."

Intuition continued, as if she'd been pent up, waiting for me to listen. "Do you really need or want to be putting all your mental energy into Journey Church, into whether it makes it or not? Or is it time for you to admit, once and for all, that you are not fond of purple shirts?" I smiled, thinking of therapist Howard's suggestion that at some point in your life, you're going to know whether or not you like purple shirts. How many years since that conversation, I wondered. Twenty-five?

Intuition was right. It was okay to be a satellite of support for Chuck, to intersect with his parishioners in ways that felt authentic to me. But it was not okay to keep putting my own needs on the back burner. I'd been spending too much time worrying about Journey, trying to brainstorm with Chuck how to grow it, how to make it support him salarywise. Trying to help him find a day job so he could do Journey on the side. And otherwise taking in all the freelance writing, editing, and online teaching that I possibly could to keep us at least half-afloat financially. I needed to get back to being just me: lover of family and friends; lover of nature; writer and artist; someone who experiences a mystical connection to the divine when immersed in nature's beauty.

"The privilege of a lifetime is being who you are," wrote Joseph Campbell, prolific author and scholar of myths and religions.

Basking in nature, making stuff, hanging with family and friends—that's who I was.

I walked back to the car, centered by my quiet outdoor hour in nature's church.

Late that afternoon I drove to the memorial service for Mary at Journey Church. The church was fuller than ever, with dozens of bodies packed into the medium-sized room in a commercial strip mall. Tom's acoustic guitar music filled the room with songs like "Forever Young" and "Stand by Me."

Chuck greeted everyone who walked in the door. He was in his element, helping Mary's people honor their sweet mother, sister, aunt, and friend. He was his usual kind, hospitable self, helping others through a difficult time.

His privilege of a lifetime.

I sought out family members—Mary's brothers, her son-in-law, her daughters—and introduced myself, telling them how well-loved Mary was by the church members.

Tom's playing stopped and Chuck delivered a short message with his special blend of humor, sensitivity, and hope. Then he invited the group to tell stories about Mary.

A friend told how silly she could be. How she liked to greet the big stuffed panda bear just inside the Java House on the west side of town.

A daughter spoke about how limited money was when they were growing up, with Mary a single mom and so little money for extras. About Mary buying her daughters snow boots for sledding but rigging up duct-taped footwear for herself. She wasn't going to miss out on the fun just because she couldn't afford boots of her own.

Her brother from Kentucky related Mary telling him on the phone about Journey Church. "They accept me for who I am," she had said.

The picture slowly emerged of the many ways Mary was connected to her tribes of family, coworkers, friends. That's the gift of a well-orchestrated memorial service; it is one of my mate's many talents to make that happen.

More guitar music from Tom, and then he played while the group sang "This Little Light of Mine," and then we blew bubbles into the air to signify the release of Mary's spirit. Then the daughters put Mary's collection of angels on two tables. "Take one in memory of Mom," they said.

I waited until the crowd had picked through the angels, and then I choose one of the leftovers: a small, silver one imprinted with the message "Angels shall guard thee."

I would hang it in the church in honor of Mary's sacred space.

Silently, I asked the angel: Will you watch over Chuck and Journey Church? Because as of today, I am resigning as primary worrier about this place.

I was resigning from being a minister's wife too. Few would notice. I would still lead book discussions and meditation groups and do other things I felt nudged to do. But otherwise, I was not going to think about this place so much.

I would just be Chuck's wife. Not the minister's wife.

I wanted to finish up this memoir and move onto other book ideas. And drawing and painting. I thought of Sally, the older woman I met when I was a nineteen-year-old undergrad and worked as a waitress at Howard Johnson's. Sally had returned to the university to study art. She wore a red bandana and created large abstract paintings. I'd always said I wanted to do something like that someday. It was time to get serious about my art learning curve.

I wanted to start more days with hikes in green spaces around Iowa City. I wanted to visit more state and national parks.

I wanted to connect with family and friends in ways that time and money would allow.

I would be sixty the following summer. Wasn't it about time to be more of who I was?

It was a privilege of a lifetime, and as Mary's sudden death reminded me, a privilege not to be taken for granted.

CHAPTER 19

River City Wild

2015–18

ITS HEYDAY WAS DECADES PAST.

Mason City once thrived as an agricultural and industrial center in north central Iowa, but the previous forty years had been tough. Along with the city's leaking population—28,000 from a high of 30,643 in 1960—the decline cast a shadow. Dozens of empty industrial buildings lined city entrances from every direction. Houses with boarded windows and unkempt yards flanked the downtown. Wary dogs tethered to chains could be spotted here and there. A nearly deserted, nondescript mall with a dying Younkers and an abandoned JCPenney sat as a 1980s anachronism in the middle of underused downtown storefronts built in the early 1900s. Retail, in the form of stand-alone big box stores and aging strip malls, had gravitated to Highway 18 on the west side of town. Vacancies had drifted that way too.

Yet another town that did not easily lift the heart.

In March of 2015, Chuck and I prepared to move to Mason City for his job with First Congregational United Church of Christ. I described the town's rough spots and confessed my discouragement to a friend, also a trailing spouse with a history of multiple moves.

"Find a house you love," she said. "You love the house first. Then you learn to love the town."

Inside, I rolled my eyes.

But on our third trip to look for housing, we checked into the Park Inn in downtown Mason City and admired Frank Lloyd

Wright's signature horizontal lines, cantilevered roofs, and art glass windows. We smiled at the tall clerk whose head nearly touched the low ceiling in the reception desk area, though the high-ceilinged, light-filled lobby just behind would have dwarfed him.

Wright was commissioned to design the Park Inn—the only Frank Lloyd Wright hotel in the world still standing—along with a connected bank and law offices, all completed in 1910. By the early 2000s, the deteriorated hotel had made the list of the top ten most endangered historic properties in Iowa. At the last minute, a local nonprofit organization, Wright on the Park, Inc., saved the hotel from demolition and spearheaded an $18.5 million renovation. Since 2011, the hotel has hosted visitors from all over the world.

The next morning Chuck and I jogged from the hotel past the stately public library and a Tudor mansion labeled MacNider Art Museum, which houses a small but impressive American art collection. We ran across the arched Meredith Willson Bridge, spanning magnificent bluffs along a large creek that feeds the Winnebago River. The bridge is named after the hometown creator of *The Music Man*, who modeled the fictitious River City after Mason City.

We passed large square houses with inviting porches that abutted the creek, not knowing we were in the Rock Crest-Rock Glen Historic District—the country's most compact grouping of Prairie School-style houses. One was designed by Wright, seven others by his colleagues. These, the hotel, and many other historic homes place Mason City on lists of the world's most architecturally interesting cities.

There was beauty and history in Mason City after all. And though I didn't yet know the details, the community had worked hard to preserve it.

Rock Crest-Rock Glen was beyond our price range, but our real estate agent showed us a modest two-story, painted-white brick home in the oak-lined Forest Park neighborhood a mile west of downtown. Built in 1939 in International style, the house was a simple rectangular cube with large windows on all sides. Two geometric frosted-glass windows, one above the other, ornamented the front entrance. Upstairs were three bedrooms with handsome wooden floors. One I could easily visualize as a best-ever office for my work as a writer and teacher. Downstairs, a cozy den's picture windows revealed a parklike backyard of large trees—now with bare, lacy branches. Behind the kitchen, a screened porch promised summer meals under the tree canopy. We read it in each other's eyes: We'd found a house to love.

In this neighborhood of homes—Tudor, Craftsman, Foursquare, Prairie, Colonial—neighbors welcomed us with breads, cookies, and invitations to summer block parties and Christmas gatherings. A couple who had lived there for over fifty years gave us a poem by Arthur Guiterman with the lines "Bless the door that opens wide/To stranger, as to kin." They said we could count on a beer any time we stopped by if we waited until after *Jeopardy!* was over at 5:00 p.m.

Indeed—bless the door that opens wide.

During spring 2016, at the beginning of our second year in Mason City, the *Globe Gazette* announced that city officials, without warning to residents, were finishing plans for a $245 million pork processing plant to be built just south of Mason City by Prestage Farms, a large-scale pork and turkey producer based in North Carolina. Owner Ron Prestage projected he'd hire 2,000 workers to process 10,000 hogs a day. Soon after, the *Des Moines Register* ran the headline, "Pork Plant Bringing Whole Lotta Hogs to Mason City," as if the project were already a done deal.

Local economic development staff, city officials, and state leaders—including then-governor Terry Branstad—were poised to give Prestage $22 million in tax incentives. Due to an aging population and low unemployment rates, most new workers and their families would be from Bosnia, the Democratic Republic of the Congo, Central America, and Southeastern Asia.

Mason Citians I talked to liked the idea of adding population, and I did too. The town needed more people, and immigrants had helped the town thrive in earlier days. In 1925, people from thirty-six countries, including Germany, Mexico, Denmark, Norway, Russia, and Sweden, lived in Mason City. Three thousand were from Greece. Iowa entrepreneur John Pappajohn is the son of Greek immigrants who came to Mason City in the early 1900s. Pappajohn, who built his fortune in insurance and venture capitalism, bequeathed millions to Iowa universities and colleges.

Everyone wanted to see the town bustle again. In 1899 Jacob Decker and Sons built a packing plant on the north side, which for a time became nearly a community unto itself with cafés and grocery stores. Armour and Co. purchased the business in 1935. At its peak, the plant employed 1,300 and processed 30,000 hogs per week. "It could be smelly," older Mason Citians told me, "but workers earned decent wages, bought homes, and supported families." Most people seemed to know someone who had made a good living at the packing plant. In 1975 Armour closed the plant due to the high cost of replacing obsolete equipment. The company had also been cited for air pollution violations.

Pollution was a big red flag for me. The prospect of a slaughterhouse just a few miles south of our home took me back to growing up on the west side of Iowa Falls and, when on the east side, smelling the putrid odor emanated by Farmland Foods, located a few miles northeast of town. When my father, brother, sister, and I went golfing at the little public course on the east side, the creek running through the course smelled as if animal parts and waste had been dumped directly into the water. At the time, everyone accepted the odor—"the smell of money," people used to say—but years later I would wonder how many people were sickened by air and water pollution from Farmland Foods.

Air, water, and soil pollution were the main concerns of an increasing number of us at the Mason City council meetings. "How would 2.8 million gallons of water a day drawn from the Jordan Aquifer affect local water supplies?" we asked. "Would the city's water be safe to drink?" New technologies might reduce the smells of rendering the hogs inside the plant, but with lines of semi-trucks waiting to unload thousands of animals per day, wouldn't prevailing winds blow hog particulates and odor into the town? Why hadn't city leaders undertaken an unbiased environmental and health study regarding the impact of slaughtering 10,000 hogs a day just south of city center?

We were also concerned about CAFOs—confined animal feeding operations—that were proliferating across north central Iowa. Prestage said his company had no need for more because it already owned hogs in the state and just needed a place to process the meat. But wouldn't other area slaughterhouses, including a new one going up in Sioux City, need additional hogs since they were losing the Prestage animals? Didn't that mean more CAFOs? Farmers needed to make a living and hog manure is good field fertilizer, but what about the manure and commercial fertilizer runoff that pollutes Iowa's waters? And what about the fact that concentrated livestock production was clearly contributing to climate change?

Why couldn't our state put a moratorium on CAFO permits until we figured out how many hogs were too many hogs?

Chuck, out of courtesy to his parishioners who were divided, refrained from weighing in on the project. Instead, he opened the church for two town meetings to let people talk about their visions and hope for Mason City. However, other townspeople and I wrote letters to editors of local and state newspapers. Attendance at city council meetings exploded, overrunning the library auditorium and spilling over into a large common space where we watched the proceedings via live TV.

Hundreds of us were there on the night of the final city council meeting. The mayor, firmly in favor of Prestage, was unable to vote; a tie among the six council members would kill the deal. Mason Citians made impassioned pleas for six hours, mostly to vote "no" because of environmental and health issues. At 2:00 a.m., three of the six council members voted against the project, heeding the vocal opposition and citing their own concerns about whether tax rebates to Prestage would cost the city more than the project would contribute. The deal was off.

Ron Prestage called Mason City slaughterhouse opponents "racist" and "kooks," in the *Des Moines Register*, trying to smear the opposition by blaming the rejection on anti-immigration sentiment. I never heard a single racist or anti-immigrant word spoken. Our resistance was about the environment. Did that make us kooks? If so, I thought we needed more kooks in Iowa to keep CAFOs from taking over the state.

Prestage Farms went on to court Eagle Grove, a town of 3,500 seventy miles southwest of Mason City. It agreed to host a Prestage plant that opened in early 2019. After that agreement, many new CAFO permits were approved in the surrounding region.

The controversy continued to rile Mason Citians, but for me, sweet lingered on with the bitter because of the community bonds we formed. We were young and old, grandparents and teenagers and community college students. We were new and longtime residents and people from out of state considering moving to Mason City. We were sustainable ag activists and union members and health professionals. We had chatted on social media and before the council meetings and afterward in the library parking lot. As I witnessed my fellow citizens' heated love of north central Iowa, their "trouble in River City" speeches, and picket signs in front of City Hall, I found them more and more endearing. And I became one of them.

Not long after the "no" vote, Chuck and I went to a local bar to hear a favorite musician play. A woman rushed over and stepped in between Chuck and me. She forced a sloppy hug upon him, nearly pinning him against the wall in the crowded room. Then she turned and proudly told her friends, "THIS man helped stop the Prestage deal."

"Saved" by the diplomatic pastor who had stayed neutral. I looked at him and rolled my eyes. He waited for the woman in between us to step away.

In downtown Mason City's Central Park, across the street from the Park Inn, a life-sized bronze statue of Frank Lloyd Wright faces the hotel. He's wearing his characteristic pork pie hat and cape. At the base of the statue are his words, "Invest in Beauty." Some days I wondered what Wright would think of the sprawling factories sitting empty on the edges of town or the houses and storefronts still boarded up. On those days, his words had an ironic ring.

But on other days, like during spring bird migration season when I spotted a scarlet tanager in Parker's Woods, a quarter-mile strip of forest just a couple blocks away from our house, I thought there should be a corresponding quote near the Wright statue that says, "Allow Beauty." "Allowing" in Mason City meant minimal manicuring due to a lack of resources. But one thing this place did well for natural beauty was to allow it.

The wild was everywhere in Mason City. It was in the fecund, overgrown hiking trail behind the Mason City Public Library. It was along the same Willow Creek that the Prairie School houses abut downstream. In the many wetlands spilled over from creeks and little prairie pothole lakes that dotted neighborhoods. In the 440-acre timber sanctuary, restored prairie, and limestone bluffs of Lime Creek Nature Center and

Conservation Area just north of town, donated by two cement companies. In town there were East Park, Georgia Hanford Park Arboretum, and Big Blue Lake, a former quarry, where people liked to dive and swim. Mason City's green spaces were rough and tumble, to be sure, but they were overflowing with nature's beauty.

If you spent enough time in these areas, you might get the impression that Mother Nature was truly more in control of Mason City than Mason City, and you would begin to appreciate her aesthetics. Spring woodland flowers held their own in vacant lots with garlic mustard plants. Ducks waddled out onto broken asphalt paths from under an old railroad bridge. Migrating trumpeter swans landed in temporary wetlands just north of an elementary school.

About a dozen years earlier, I had interviewed an Iowan named Roger Gipple for an article I had pitched to a magazine. Gipple was a retired farmer and environmentalist who lived in Des Moines and had established the Agrestal Fund, which for a time helped generate a statewide dialogue about wildness in Iowa by sponsoring interdisciplinary conferences on the wild at Iowa State and the University of Iowa.

Gipple told me he liked the word "agrestal" because it means "not domesticated or cultivated; growing wild in the field." Inspired by Thoreau's famous line "In wildness is the preservation of the world," Gipple felt that as our landscape continues to shift from large tracts of unspoiled nature (what we think of as "wilderness") toward more urban areas, we will need to value small places of "wildness" in the city, like flowers growing between the cracks of sidewalks and raptors dwelling in urban trees. Wildness is an experience available to us all whether in rural or urban settings.

Because of Gipple's ideas, I have made efforts, wherever we have lived, to get to know the local places of wildness. That's why the half-neglected green spaces around Mason City suited me just fine, such as when I ran along the Winnebago River and spotted a heron spreading prehistoric wings and taking flight downriver. It comforted me that right here in River City, patches of woods and grasses were allowed to go a little wild. As it turned out, I was proud to live in an agrestal town growing wild in the middle of acres and acres of corn, soybeans, and CAFOS in north central Iowa.

Roger Gipple told me those years ago that wildness was also a metaphor. "It's a self-reliant, spontaneous, liberated state," he said. I had begun to reclaim my own wildness, liberating myself more often from writing deadlines to learn to paint and draw, or to daydream and think about ideas and the environment and people. People like Roger Gipple, whom I met just a couple of times, but whose thoughts about wildness live on in my mind.

Or people like my townmates, who showed their wild sides of anger and commitment as they stood up for their right to fresh air and clean water. People who gathered in increasing numbers once a month as members of the Citizen Climate Advocates of North Central Iowa to learn about climate change and to lobby legislators with letters and phone calls. People, including a new mayor and a mostly new city council, who were hard at work on a River City Renaissance Project that could revive the downtown with a new hockey arena, hotel, and events center. Some worried this project was a house of cards, and maybe it was. But my fellow citizens were a scrappy bunch. If it didn't work, they'd get behind something else, just as they had rescued the almost-buried treasure of the Park Hotel in the nick of time. Just as they had taken a stand against potential environmental threats from corporate agriculture.

Gipple equated wildness with a kind of mysticism, a "spiritual fuel," he said, which he could find "with my back to an oak tree in the city, or even in bed at night. There's a larger, ongoing thing—a wildness—of which I am a part." I could feel that connection too, sometimes, like while working on the porch and watching a half-dozen Baltimore orioles spatting over the grape jelly in our feeder just above our chemical-free, half-wild yard.

I was also lucky to feel connected to my community, and not just to the living. I felt it with Frank Lloyd Wright and his colleagues William Drummond, Walter Burley Griffin, Frances Barry Bryne, and countless other architects who had left thumbprints on homes that had been lovingly preserved around town. I felt it with Meredith Willson, whose "Seventy-Six Trombones" was played at every Memorial Day parade, and with Willson's sister, Dixie, an author, poet, and screenwriter whose legacy was also carefully tended in the community. I felt it with Chuck's parishioners, who sweetly accepted me even though they had come to understand that I was not a church lady.

With each of our four moves in the past sixteen years, I had left friends and family behind and become confused about where home really was. But I counted myself especially lucky to feel these connections in Mason City—to the wild, to history, to beauty, to creativity, and to community.

Sometimes these connections were enough.

Sometimes they were everything.

CHAPTER 20

Skipping Church

2018

DESPITE MY GROWING CONTENTMENT IN MASON CITY, ONE or two Sundays a month in the pew at First Congregational United Church of Christ was still a lot for a girl who is spiritual but not religious, even if it was her handsome husband with the dimples in the pulpit. I enjoyed Chuck's dear parishioners, but attending church, for me, was still an itchy skin ready to be shed. Missing the weekly sangha that I had attended in Iowa City, I decided on a cold Sunday in March to skip church and get up early to drive two hours to the Zen Meditation Center in southwest Minneapolis—the nearest Buddhist center. Maybe it was the place to restart my learning curve in Buddhism.

The Center, near Lake Calhoun, is a white, boxy, two story building with a crumbling stone walkway. The small vestibule was crowded with about twenty people standing quietly, waiting for the meditation hour to end. I was already hooked by their silence, maybe because of the DNA I share with Quaker ancestors. I removed my boots, placing them neatly beside the other footwear lined up along two walls. The tops flopped down, taking up extra space. I let them be.

Soon the doors slid open, revealing two large rooms. On the right, what was once surely a living room was covered with pads and zafus—round meditation pillows. To my left, the dining area held a dozen chairs in rows facing the living room. Some people were already sitting with their eyes closed; others were milling around on the creaky wooden floors, quietly greeting each other. A few had handmade biblike cloths around their necks. I learned later that meditators present these rakusus to lay practitioners as part of an initiation ceremony.

I headed left and took a chair. Soon a bald man entered the room. Bussho Lahn (*Bussho* is Japanese for "Buddha-nature") began his talk by telling us that we all held the dharma within, which meant he would simply be reminding us of things we already knew.

I sighed, already feeling at home.

He said religious scholar Huston Smith, when asked what the ordinary nonreligious American might miss by not aligning to a religious tradition, replied, "*Sat, chit,* and *ananda*: 'infinite being, infinite awareness, infinite bliss.' Does the ordinary, decent, secular American aspire to that? Does he see it as within his register? There is a special circle in Dante's hell that is populated by souls whose only fault was that their aspirations were too low."

One way we keep our aspirations low, said Bussho Lahn, is by what we take for granted. We also get attached to our suffering: We think of loneliness as "my loneliness." Instead, he said, we might say, "I am experiencing the loneliness." We also grasp for what we do not have—one of our main sources of suffering. "But giving up our grasping can be seen as an act of generosity," he said.

I wondered which of my many graspings to try to relax. That old, nagging wish to return to Iowa City's rolling hills and sangha and friends with whom I once thought I would grow old? The desire to quit my day job as an adjunct online university instructor watching student enrollments increase without corresponding pay increases? The longing to see more of our California grandsons, already half-grown?

Let the feelings come, my inner dharma said. Accept them with compassion and nonjudgment, and then let them go. At least for now. Who knows what the future holds? Okay to want. Not okay to grasp—unless you want to suffer.

After the talk I mingled, and as I left, I offered to help an elderly lady down the few steps to the sidewalk. She said she was fine, just slow. "I can't get here anymore as often as I would like," she told me as we stepped down side by side. "But I always enjoy it when I can come." I admired her acceptance of the what-is—her nongrasping.

It was still cold and the wind bit. I gave up on the plan to walk three miles around Lake Calhoun and, instead, drove to the nearby Minneapolis Institute of Art. Along the way, I savored the feeling of being fed by Bussho Lahn's dharma talk. I didn't feel guilty, like I once might have, at not being in the pew for Chuck's sermon that morning. I just felt grateful.

There was a small exhibit of Chinese Buddhist art at the Minnesota Institute of Art. I read from a sign on the wall: "Buddhism, one of China's three major belief systems, was imported from India along the overland trade corridor during the first century B.C. Like the indigenous philosophies of Confucianism and Taoism, Buddhism honored no supreme deity." For over a thousand years, Buddhist communities were major patrons of monumental sculpture, painting, printing, and temple architecture—art that absorbed various foreign, religious, and philosophical influences. The Buddhist art of Tibet produced complex mandalas and ritual objects. A meditative branch of Chinese Buddhism known as Chan (Zen in Japan), which favored sudden enlightenment through meditation over scriptural learning, produced more-intuitive, expressive paintings.

My neurons lit up. Enlightenment over scriptural learning. Bingo. That was me. I still most often experienced enlightenment when walking alone in the woods or on a prairie while just naturally meditating on the sights and sounds around me. Enlightenment, intuition, insight—perhaps they were one and the same—often guided my creative work in writing and art. Why I couldn't experience these feelings in a Christian church the way Chuck did was beyond me. Certainly, life would be easier for both of us if I could, I thought for the thousandth time. But at least I felt enlightenment—transcendence—and on a regular basis. For that I was incredibly lucky.

In another section of the museum, people were clustered around a sculpture called *Rendezvous*, created in 1981 from Indiana limestone by Apache artist Allan Houser (1914–1994). Hanging on the wall behind the sculpture was a colorful, woven Native American blanket. The Buddhist statues and artifacts were fresh in my mind, and the contrast of the smooth, white monochromatic sculpture against the bold colors of the blanket transfixed me. I stood there, drinking it all in, and then it happened: that mystical feeling that everything is connected and that I was part of the universal whole. That invisible, mystical river again. I soaked it up for the two or three minutes that it lasted.

Sat, chit, ananda. Infinite being, infinite awareness, infinite bliss.

Enlightenment.

I was not looking for it. I was not grasping. It just happened.

Several days later, while using the photo I took to draw and paint the sculpture and blanket with pen and gouache, I experienced it all over again: Being. Awareness. Bliss.

There are so many good ways to raise our aspirations. We should count ourselves lucky if we find them. Even if it means skipping church.

CHAPTER 21

It Takes Two

2018

ON A COLD WINTER EVENING IN MASON CITY, I SUGGESTED to Chuck that the next summer we should head two hours north to Minneapolis for dance lessons. "You know how much I've wanted to learn the tango," I said. "A studio offers it on Tuesdays at 7 p.m. We could knock off work midafternoon, have an early dinner at a sidewalk café, go to the lesson, and be home by 10."

My affable mate nodded—absent-mindedly, I thought. So I amped up the pitch. "Remember how I used to joke that if it comes time to die, and I have gone to church more than we have danced, I would really be pissed? Well, the joke isn't funny anymore. I know I skip church more than I used to, but I'm still in the pew way more often than we are dancing."

He smiled grimly.

"I know you prefer the salsa," I continued. "But I'd like to try the formal lessons in tango. My brain is craving that kind of learning."

"Okay. Let's do it," he said.

Later that spring I read in the church e-newsletter that Chuck had committed to spearheading a weekly fundraiser that would go all summer long; it involved cooking—his passion—and would take place on Tuesday evenings. Chuck and teams of parishioners would use a donated food truck to prepare and serve meals in conjunction with the farmers market across the street.

"Need more details?" queried the newsletter. "Just contact Pastor Chuck."

Tango trumped by food truck? Inconceivable. But there it

was, carved in e-stone, right in front of God and everyone—food truck every Tuesday evening, June through September.

That night I quizzed Pastor Chuck about the details.

"Sorry," he said, "with so many things going on, I neglected to tell you, and I'm sorry, but I had forgotten about the tango."

It didn't take long for the fundraiser to develop a minor following. Farmers market patrons bought produce and then crossed the street to the church parking lot, lured by the delicious smells of pizza, tacos, and paella from the Reverend and his gang. People talked and laughed, sitting at the tables in the shade. Chuck and the volunteers had fun. The church was making some pin money. There was a sense of community, and the church was attracting the attention of potential newcomers. Who could argue with that?

Surely not the pastor's wife.

I helped a few times on food truck Tuesdays, but as the summer went on, I lost heart and stopped, yet scolded myself for it. This was just one extra evening commitment on Chuck's part. And really, how could I begrudge any of the ways Chuck was serving here in Mason City—and not just the church but the community itself. People appreciated the way he'd established weekly meditation and discussion groups for those who weren't churchgoers but still needed a sense of belonging. He helped other groups get off the ground too: a bipolar support group and a caregivers assistance group. He supported the LGBTQ+ community with his welcoming presence, offering church space for events.

I wasn't twiddling my thumbs. I helped organize monthly meetings for the Citizens Climate Advocates of North Central Iowa. I led a mindfulness/meditation workshop for the church and taught a couple writing and art classes for the community college adult-ed program. I joined book groups and a study group and helped host a neighborhood women's group. I was in conversation with a few people about starting up a sangha to meet in someone's home.

So why was I taking Chuck's additional Tuesday evening commitment so hard? Why couldn't I just get over it?

One Tuesday evening in late July, feeling low about the summer's disappointment, I stayed home and read from Buddhist teacher Tara Brach's book *True Refuge*. In the chapter "Losing What We Love: The Pain of Separation," she wrote that "we may carry a hidden grief for years."

Food truck Tuesdays opened the wound of old losses that come with being married to a pastor—losses that are invisible to most. Our moves across Iowa and repeatedly losing easy access to friends. Having to leave Iowa City with its rolling hills and cultural vibrancy that always lifted my heart. The loss of Chuck's companionship to meetings and programs, concerns and crises, and the preferences and accolades of parishioners.

After all these years I couldn't readily admit these losses without sounding selfish, even to myself. But when we suffer a loss, Brach says, we should resist self-blame and hold ourselves kindly. "Meet our edge and soften," she advises.

I took deep breaths, let myself feel the grief I'd kept mostly hidden and silent for so many years, and faced my edge. My heart overflowed with emotion. All the years I had felt like a single parent with a demanding career of my own that got regularly trumped by the church calendar. All the times I sat, quiet and invisible, at get-to-know-you dinners with parishioners who only had eyes for Chuck as they doled out the questions: How long have you been in ministry? How did you know you wanted to be a minister? What did you do before you became a minister? Do you wear a robe? What do you think about . . . ? All the times I sat by myself at weddings and funerals while my husband officiated. All the Sunday mornings I reached outside of my agnosticism and attended church to be supportive to my husband and his congregation, yet in the pew without him at my side. All the times I felt alone and rejected and unloved and cast aside by Chuck in favor of those whose needs seemed greater or more pressing or maybe just more interesting than my own.

Oh, how I identified with that agrestal flower mentioned by Roger Gipple all those years earlier, that flower growing between the cracks of a sidewalk. The perseverance that wasn't cultivated, wasn't planned, wasn't nurtured, wasn't manicured by the kinds of resources that would help that flower grow. The flower that was half-neglected, often overlooked—just allowed. The little bit of wildness coloring outside the lines, growing between the cracks of a vast sidewalk called Church with all its requisite demands on a pastor, and on a marriage, and on the lonely life of one who stands outside its paradigm.

Yes, I felt it, the grief, and the way the years of accumulated losses had settled in my throat and chest and shoulders.

Breathe, Suzanne. I told myself. Breathe. It takes a strong partner to live with the realities of being married to a minister.

But I am not always strong.

I put my hand over my heart.

Marriage entails sacrifice, the late mythologist Joseph Campbell told Bill Moyers in *The Power of Myth*, a book based on a series of interviews on public television. "Marriage is not a simple love affair, it's an ordeal," he said. "And the ordeal is the sacrifice of ego to a relationship in which two have become one."

I'd held on to a copy of Campbell's words all these years, just to remind myself that I didn't want my ego to constrain our marriage or Chuck's need to answer his calling. Becoming a pastor was a natural evolution of who he was, and if he couldn't be who he was because of me, then I would be hurting both him and me.

Hold yourself kindly, Suzanne.

Meet your edge and soften.

Brach offers wisdom from Sri Nigargadatta, an Indian teacher, on handling loss: "The mind creates the abyss. The heart crosses over it."

I well knew our marriage held sacrifices for Chuck too. He rarely complained of the difficulty in balancing the needs of his parishioners while also trying to be there as a husband and father. It had to be tough to have a wife who didn't share his theology, who found it difficult to transition to each new community. He surely felt overwhelmed at times, yet he was so steady and uncomplaining.

On this lonely Tuesday evening, I had to admit it: My mind had at least partially created this current abyss. Didn't Chuck show his love in so many ways, from bringing flowers in from the garden, to foot massages while we watched TV, to delicious home-cooked meals for two on our porch? True, his loving was often tucked in between church goings-on. But I knew he loved me.

How was I to cross over this abyss that had opened the wound of old losses?

"Sense who you most want to feel love from," Brach advises, "and when someone comes to mind, visualize that person right here and ask . . . say the words, 'Please love me.' You might then imagine what it would be like to receive love, just the way you want it." In this way, she suggests, we tap into the deeper love that unites us all, even when we're feeling apart from that love.

It all made sense. But why should I have to imagine my husband's love?

What I wanted was his presence. And not just on the fly. Over the winter I had asked him to put tango lessons on his calendar. He'd agreed. Then, like Charlie Brown's friend Lucy, he'd moved the football.

That night, Chuck arrived home high on food truck love. I said nothing about my dismal evening, my mind still in the abyss.

The next morning I asked him, gently as possible, to consider giving up one food truck night in mid-August to head with me to Minneapolis for one tango lesson. "You've got the fundraiser underway now," I said. "Maybe it would be good for your team to take over once in a while."

Please love me, Chuck, my heart said silently.

"Let me see what I can do," he said.

After a few more food truck Tuesdays, Minneapolis Tuesday finally arrived. Summer had fluctuated between oppressively hot or unseasonably cool, but this day was warm and sunny. He had researched restaurants near the area, settling on a Latin fusion café with outdoor seating. I tried not to feel like I'd begged for Chuck's attention but wondered if he resented taking time away from his cooking and community-building. We ordered wine and a light meal of veggie empanadas and braised scallops. We'd been married forty-two years, but this night we were two shy people just getting to know each other.

After our meal we headed to the Four Seasons Dance Studio, in an historic building near the Walker Art Center. In the studio was a baby grand piano and torn overstuffed furniture strewn around the edges of a scuffed wooden floor. Bruce, the instructor, greeted us and asked us to introduce ourselves. Soon we were walking in a circle with smooth strides, feet not far apart, moving forward gracefully, trying not to bob. Bruce taught us to walk in pairs, holding onto each other with strong arms, leaders guiding with their hands and bodies.

We began practicing ochos—followers making figure eights with leaders standing in place. Chuck wore jeans and an open-collared shirt. With my solid rubber-soled sandals, I wasn't ochoing very smoothly in my flippy black skirt and glitzy tank top, but I didn't care. As the short, oldest lady with the salt-and-pepper hair, I was beginning to feel alive after the trying summer. My mate seemed comfortable too.

As we followed Bruce's directions, we began to learn the tango form—its constraints and possibilities. It was like practicing the clarinet in my youth: trying something new, repeating and drilling the lesson into muscle memory so that eventually it could be done without thinking. I felt old neuronal paths begin to light up. Chuck may have missed his food truck high that night, but I was tango-high all the way home.

As he headed out the door to work the next morning, I felt the abyss rising again. I couldn't help myself: I wanted more. I'd hoped he would suggest another lesson on the way home. But there had been no mention of tango, and now it was back to his regular church commitments.

"Wait," I said. "I know I am pressing my luck, but how would you feel about going up again next week? Two lessons in a row could help cement our learning just a little bit. And then I wouldn't ask for more this summer."

He looked like he wanted to roll his eyes, like he'd been expecting my question, like he felt a little guilty that he hadn't offered.

Please love me, my heart said.

"I'll see what I can do."

The next week we decided to stay overnight in Minneapolis since it was close to my sixty-third birthday. This time there were five or six couples. I was ready with new smooth-soled shoes, black capri leggings, and a red dress. Chuck wore dress pants and a button-down shirt. My handsome husband.

Bruce had us repeat parts of the previous week's lesson, then introduced a few more steps, encouraging the men to be firmer about their leads and the women to exaggerate the slant of their hips during the figure-eight ochos. The music was traditional tango-style with the accordion, but in my mind, we were dancing to the hard-driving beat of a Latin dance club.

Slow, slow, quick slow.

"There are two completely different stages of marriage," Joseph Campbell told Bill Moyers. "First is the youthful marriage, during which we follow the wonderful impulses that nature has given us in the interplay of the sexes biologically in order to produce children.

"Sometimes," he continued, "there becomes beautifully realized in the second stage of marriage what I call the alchemical stage, of the two experiencing that they are one."

Slow, slow, quick, quick slow.

As we practiced, I imagined us gliding effortlessly through the steps—and through the years: our first date at fifteen, clinging to each other while "Hey Jude" played at the Christmas dance; the long, cold winter walk home from the high school that made his nose run during our first kiss; riding around the county on his motorcycle, our bodies nestled close, my arms around his waist; our wedding on a cold night in January during our junior year in college; a few years later, reluctantly moving back to our hometown with my heart in my throat; a beautiful baby boy, and then another, equally perfect; flying kites with them on a hill above the Iowa River Valley.

Slow, slow, side step slow. Arguments in our twenties and thirties as we hashed out who we were individually and who we were together.

The proclamation in our apartment living room that changed our lives forever—his decision to become a minister. Learning from my inner Bitch. Our compromises, our attempts to support each other.

Slow, slow, ocho. Our laughter. Our tears, our fears, our moves, our adaptations.

Our sons, their mates, their adventures. A wedding in California, a vivacious new daughter-in-law. Our grandsons. Our working together as a team to care for them as they got older and visited us in Iowa summers. Swimming at a lake and the municipal pool, biking and hiking, tennis and breakfast at the Suzie-Q diner. Another wedding in Mexico; another lovely daughter-in-law.

Our new lives.

The hole in our hearts when we thought about the distance between us and them, all living in California, where the cost of living was too high for us to ever think about locating there.

But our good times with them, whenever possible, and many good meals at our various homes with our sibs and my mom, and with friends, old and new.

Our lows, our celebrations. Our failures, our resiliencies.

Slow, slow, ocho.

The next morning in downtown Minneapolis was lazy, and then a long lunch at an outdoor café. My appetite for tango was only whetted after our second lesson, and yet it was also satisfied. We'd reestablished our marriage in the middle of things for long enough to heal the summer's disappointment.

As he drove us toward home, Chuck gazed out at the horizon from the wheel of the Honda. "So maybe I'll line up a team again for next Tuesday," he said. "We can drive up for another tango lesson or do whatever you would like to do."

He looked at me, smiled, touched my hand. My eyes told him, Reverend, it doesn't really take much to make us right again. Occasionally, I just need to know there's an "us" in the middle of your sea of responsibilities.

I felt it now—the alchemy.

Our hearts still quickening at the sight of each other.

Our corks, always bobbing again—slow, slow, ocho, slow— even in rough waters.

CHAPTER 22

California Dreaming

2018–21

IN THE EARLY SUMMER OF 2018, WE FLEW TO CALIFORNIA to watch our grandsons for a week, and the four of us stayed at an apartment in Berkeley. One morning Chuck took the boys to a park while I headed to the UC Berkeley library to tend to a class I was teaching online for the University of Iowa. Sitting in a light-filled, spacious room at the library, soaking up the view of the beautiful Berkeley campus, surrounded by scholars intent at their own laptops, I was overcome with a tremendous, almost supernatural, feeling of well-being. I felt full of love—for the campus; for books, scholarship, and higher education; for the others in the room; for my family; and for the land and people of northern California.

To mark this mystical moment, I wrote in the "notes" section on my iPhone: "What a pleasure it could be to live in this area, see our kids and grandkids more often, and use the UC Berkeley library."

I never mentioned the experience to anyone—not even Chuck. I remembered Andrew Harvey's warning in *Dialogues with a Modern Mystic* that an addiction to mystical experiences "can end in a subtle grief, in which we are longing for bliss" and miss out on life. And as far as grasping after a chance to live in California, I agreed with the Buddhists that grasping and avoiding are two of the three main causes of suffering. The third is delusion, or foolishness. As I knew, it was foolish to ever think that living in the Bay Area would fall within our modest budget.

Besides, we were enjoying the creative, smart people in

Mason City who had welcomed us with such open arms. We lived in a house we loved and in the best neighborhood ever. We were back in marital harmony once again. Except for the dull ache of missing our family in California, life was good back in River City.

Chuck didn't tell me at first about the job he applied for on a whim in late summer. He guessed that no one west of the Missouri River would want to hire a sixty-three-year-old preacher from Iowa. In the early fall he came to me, proverbial hat in hand, and confessed he'd applied for a position at a church in San Francisco. "And apparently the parishioners like my résumé enough to request a Skype interview."

"It's a small church—a UCC a couple miles south of Golden Gate Park," he added. "The church is within a half hour of the kids, and if we lived across in the East Bay, we could be even closer."

"But how would we afford to live there?" I asked.

"Let's just see what they say," he said.

He Skyped with the San Francisco parishioners, and then we both put it out of our minds, expecting—almost hoping—that nothing would change.

Early February 2019 found us preparing for our first dinner guests in an empty apartment in Alameda, a small island city of 80,000 just south of Oakland and a few miles across the bay from San Francisco. We weren't alone together on a Sunday night in a new Iowa town, wistful about our kids so far away. It wasn't a meal for getting to know new congregants with the inevitable grilling on why Chuck decided to be a minister or what he thought about X or Y. It was a meal for our sons, our daughters-in-law, and our grandsons, served on a folding table. And it was in person, not Facetime.

As it turned out, the small San Francisco congregation did want the sixty-three-year-old preacher from Iowa with experience in growing and revitalizing churches—enough to offer a salary to cover our increased cost of living. They dangled the gift of residing within ten miles of our family, and we reached for it—but without having grasped.

That night we ate heartily and played board games and such a raucous game of hide-and-seek in the small space that the neighbor below us knocked at our door, asking us to be mindful that people lived underneath. Hearing "Mom" and "Dad" and "Gramps" and "Nana, when will we stay overnight?" will forever ring in our ears. ("As soon as the furniture arrives, dear grandsons!")

We settled into our work and wove in frequent get-togethers with family: hikes, meet-ups at restaurants and food trucks, games of Pitch and Kings Korner and Code Names and dominoes and soccer. More home-cooked meals. A Mother's Day with a walk along the bay with one son, sketching time with the other. A Father's Day pro soccer game for Chuck and sons and grandsons. A two-week visit from my mother, our offspring making time for many meals and a daylong adults-only excursion to wine country. Grandsons overnight every few weeks and more in the summer. Biking and swimming, tennis and Ping Pong.

In all, more spontaneous get-togethers with our immediate family in the first six months than since Jess had left for California seventeen years earlier.

And no plane tickets necessary.

"This is the reason I stay out here even though I can't afford it on my retirement income," said the tall, seventy-something man who, like Chuck and me, had just finished hiking the Tennessee Valley Trail in Marin County. He lived close to the trail, he told us, and hiked this big backyard daily.

It was a Friday. Chuck and I had climbed Coyote Ridge on hills shaggy with grasses. Groves of trees along a waterway led us finally to the ocean. The wild. It gave us joy, renewing us and reminding us why, besides our family, we liked it here.

We'd eaten an early lunch at a café along Shoreline Highway, grabbed a cup of Equator coffee in Mill Valley, and then had driven to this trailhead suggested by the waitress. Sunshine, mid-fifties, the land's thirst quenched by winter rains. A perfect day.

Chuck's new congregation enthusiastically encouraged him

to take Fridays off. The church was small and unexpected interruptions rare, so we embarked on our Explore Fridays. As the weekly excursions piled up, they began to compensate for the thirty years that his church schedules, commitments, and emergencies had so often trumped time for us.

We rode the ferry to Angel Island, hiked Mount Tamalpais in Marin County, tromped all over redwood forests in the Oakland and Berkeley hills. We ferried to San Francisco, had lunch with sons in the beautiful Yerba Buena Gardens, rode the city train to Golden Gate Park, took in exhibits at the deYoung art museum, walked the three miles to the western edge of the park, then down to the windy beach to walk barefoot on the fine, soft sand along the Pacific Ocean.

Adventures spilled into other days, like the Sunday afternoon we attended Lawrence Ferlinghetti's 100th birthday celebration outside City Lights Bookstore. We signed a giant birthday card and watched dozens of hippies, old and young, greet each other as if they all lived in a small town. There were outdoor salsa dancing opportunities, lectures, and concerts all over the Bay Area.

With our move west I knew we would relish the times with our family. What I didn't anticipate was the healing we would experience in our marriage as we devoted a day a week to these adventures and explorations.

To us.

I had always loved my husband. What I didn't know was that with Explore Fridays, I would fall in love with him all over again.

Joseph Campbell's alchemy. The heart crossing the abyss, à la Tara Brach.

A happy ending.

A new beginning.

In March of 2020, fourteen months after our arrival to the area, COVID-19 became a household word and quickly throttled down our family time and explorations. As I write this in July 2021, the pandemic rages on, though vaccines now hold promise.

Chuck and I count ourselves especially lucky to be here during this pandemic. If we still lived in Iowa, we'd have been wondering when we'd ever see our Bay Area loved ones again.

My indomitable husband looks for ways to grow the church despite the circumstances. He uses Zoom for one-to-one conversations or small-group gatherings. On Sundays he drives across the bay to the empty church to film the service live on Facebook with the sanctuary as the backdrop. "It gives comfort to the parishioners," he says.

Gatherings at churches are considered risky behavior during this pandemic, but one of the healthiest and least risky things to do is get outdoors for exercise and time in nature. Trees, we are told by biologists, release certain aromatic compounds that improve our immunity, and we all know the calming effect of walking beside a body of water.

Yes, my lifelong preference for being in nature over church is now officially justified.

Along with COVID-19, other events are changing the way we do things in this world, giving us a chance, if we take it, to reimagine how best to live. The strengthening Black Lives Matter movement is demanding true justice, for once and for all, after years of oppression. From classrooms and offices to CAFOs and packing plants, we are questioning how many in one space is too many. COVID-19 and the corresponding economic freefall have caused us to work remotely when possible and slow our fuel consumption levels, giving Mother Nature a break but also urging us toward a world that casts wider, kinder, and more generous social nets for those who struggle because of color or class, capability or country.

It is easy to be pessimistic at this time, harder to hope against hope that, together, we can figure this out. To fuel optimism, each morning I attend the Church of Open Sea and Sky, located just outside our apartment along the San Francisco Bay on a several-mile path in Alameda. Across the bay to the south, I can see the hills of San Francisco. Around the bend to the west, I see the downtown San Francisco cityscape, including the monster Salesforce Tower that sits mostly idle. Along the water, different varieties of flowers seem to blossom every day, beckoning me to continue learning a whole new vocabulary. At low tide, brown pelicans, egrets, night herons, and other shore birds harvest fish and mollusks, crustaceans and insects.

As I walk, sometimes I imagine what might be happening in an Iowa prairie at the same time of year. Maybe the ragwort is in bloom, or blazing star, or bright orange milkweed. Maybe the purple coneflowers are poking out of the summer prairie grasses.

Before long, the bluestem will ripen into its lovely mauves and purples; soon after, it will go brown and poke out of the snow. About that time, here in the East Bay, if we're lucky, winter rains will turn the brown grasses back into green.

Nature. That's still where I sense the divine presence most deeply. The divine voice.

She tells me that while it's not up to me to solve all of society's ills, I can certainly add my voice to the demands of justice and health care for all. I can make my voice heard about climate change. I can do my best to remember that we are all deeply connected to and dependent upon Nature.

She reminds me that I have supported Chuck in the best way that I could; that, in turn, Chuck has supported me in my callings as a writer and a teacher, and maybe even as an artist if I keep working at it, which shouldn't be hard to do with so many artists living and teaching in northern California.

She celebrates with me this time in our lives to be active grandparents to grandsons, even though the pandemic is still slowing us down for now. She rejoices that there is now a third grandson—a brand-new baby boy. That though we'll likely retire in Iowa where the cost of living is more reasonable, we do have a few precious years here to lovingly watch our grandchildren's lives unfold.

She's happy that with a few more salsa lessons after sheltering-in-place ends, even Chuck's and my dancing skills may start to come along quite nicely. (Good compromise on salsa, she says; he was never going to like the tango.)

She reminds me that Chuck and I have both had the privilege to be who we are. That I am lucky to be married to him, even if he marches to Gabriel's horn and I to the wind.

She reminds me, through Julian of Norwich, that "All shall be well and all shall be well and all manner of things shall be well."

That all has been well, all along, even when I didn't know it.

That wherever I've been, I have arrived.

That wherever I am, I am Home.

About the Author

Suzanne & Charles Kelsey

A recent transplant from the Midwest to northern California, Suzanne Kelsey is a writer, artist, university instructor, and a lover of family, friends, nature, contemplation, and creative pursuits.

SHANTI ARTS

NATURE ▪ ART ▪ SPIRIT

Please visit us online
to browse our entire book catalog,
including poetry collections and fiction,
books on travel, nature, healing, art,
photography, and more.

Also take a look at our highly
regarded art and literary journal,
Still Point Arts Quarterly, which
may be downloaded for free.

www.shantiarts.com

CPSIA information can be obtained
at www.ICGtesting.com
Printed in the USA
BVHW041346231121
622339BV00011B/462

9 781956 056075